YOURS ARE

THE HANDS

of CHRIST

YOURS ARE

THE HANDS

of CHRIST

THE PRACTICE
OF FAITH

JAMES C. HOWELL

UPPER
ROOM BOOKS
NASHVILLE

The Upper Room® Web address: http://www.upperroom.org

Grateful acknowledgment is expressed to the following for permission to reprint previously published material:

Random House: Excerpt from *The Place Within: The Poetry of Pope John Paul II,* tran. Jerzy Peterkiewicz ©1982. Used by permission of the publisher.

Henry Holt and Company: Excerpt from "Death of the Hired Man," from *The Poetry of Robert Frost,* ed. Edward Connery Lathem © 1958 by Robert Frost; © 1967 by Lesley Frost Ballantine; Copyright 1930, 1939, © 1969 by Henry Holt and Company. Reprinted by permission of Henry Holt and Company, Inc.

Scripture quotations are from the New Revised Standard Version of the Bible © 1989 by the Division of Christian Education of the National Council of the Churches of Christ in the USA. Used by permission. All rights reserved.

Art Direction and Cover Design: D² DesignWorks
Cover Photograph: Tony Stone Images/Andrew Olney
Interior Design: D² Designworks
Second printing: 2000

Library of Congress Cataloging-in-Publication Data

Howell, James C., 1955-
    Yours are the hands of Christ : the practice of faith / James C. Howell.
      p. cm.
    ISBN 0-8358-0867-X
    1. Christian life—Methodist authors. 2. Jesus Christ—Biography. I. Title.
BV4509.5.H   1999
248.4'876—dc21   98-38253
                                  CIP

The material in this book has been coming into being for some time. I want to express thanks to my teachers, especially Father Roland Murphy, who modelled for me how to be a student of the Bible and a lover of the church. I am grateful to the congregation at Davidson United Methodist Church, partly for listening appreciatively and critically to my preaching each Sunday, and more so for their commitment to be the hands of Christ in countless projects in our community and even in places like Lithuania, Belarus, and Guatemala.

Special thanks go to Janice Grana, executive editor at Upper Room Books, for taking on this project. I am grateful to her, and also to Holly Halverson and Glenda Webb at Upper Room, for the wonderful improvements they made in bringing the manuscript to completion. As in everything that I do, I am indebted to the diligent assistance of my secretaries, Alison Edmiston, Karen Bright, and Terrie Stark.

I am honored by and indebted to the following who read some or all of the manuscript and made helpful suggestions: Peter Krentz, professor of classics, Davidson College; Rowan Crews, professor of theology, Claflin College; Andy Baxter, my trusty associate pastor at Davidson United Methodist Church; Rabbi Jim Bennett of Temple Beth El; Rob King, pastor of the Mill Grove and Zion United Methodist Churches; Jason Byassee, student at Duke University Divinity School; and Lisa Stockton Howell, my wife, who is a voracious reader of mysteries and of all the stuff I put out.

This book is dedicated to her. Her own hands are remarkable. With them she expresses the ineffable through liturgical dance. With them she frames and hammers nails in Habitat houses. With them she does a thousand things that make our house a home and our community a better place.

Now you are the body of Christ.
(1 Cor. 12:27)

C hristians face a staggering challenge today. We must be the hands of Christ in this world. Christianity must become something real, tangible, something that pervades all that we are. It must become something we *do.*

Not that this is a new challenge. It is as old as the Bible itself. But in our culture, for Christianity to have any meaningful future, we must get serious about a genuine, flesh-and-blood lifestyle that is holy without being elitist, engaged with the world without becoming jaded by it, active and busy in the world yet prepared to cope with failure.

The challenge before us is nowhere more beautifully expressed than in these words popularly attributed to Teresa of Avila, a holy woman who lived in Spain in the sixteenth century:

> Christ has no body now on earth but yours,
> no hands but yours,
> no feet but yours.
> Yours are the eyes through which the compassion
> of Christ is to look out on a hurting world.

Yours are the feet with which he is to go about

doing good.

Yours are the hands with which he is to bless now.

In this book we will contemplate what it means to be the hands of Christ. We will explore, with some imagination and a search through the Gospels, what Jesus did with his hands, and what we are called to do with ours. We will consider saints through the centuries as well as contemporary events and literature that can help us envision the radical nature of the Christian life.

TRIED AND FOUND WANTING

Sadly, we have a dreadful tendency to let our faith remain invisible, strangely mute, just something pasted on the exterior of a life that is really no different from a non-Christian life. Little wonder people increasingly regard Christianity as irrelevant. To reach people today, we must demonstrate the seriousness, the tangibility of our faith. Among his many insightful remarks, G. K. Chesterton once said that it is not that Christianity has been tried and found wanting. Rather, it is that Christianity has hardly ever been tried.

Many Christians may swiftly remind us that we are saved by faith, not by works. A mountain of good deeds does not earn us admission into heaven. But there is far more to the Christian life than merely getting into heaven. The evangelist Billy Sunday once said that the best thing that could happen to a man would be for him to attend a revival meeting, accept Christ as his savior, and then go out and get run over and killed by a truck. But that would be to miss out on the adventure of living day in and day out as disciples of Christ. Jesus didn't dole out pithy formulas, scale metaphysical heights, or outline dogmas. Instead he talked incessantly about how to live our lives, how to spend our money, how to treat others. More importantly, he lived a unique life, had no money, and touched others in exemplary ways.

I have written this book as a reminder of how utterly mundane it is to be a Christian. We need to hear the historic summons to "be doers of the word, and not merely hearers" (James 1:22). If we are honest, we admit that we are often the latter. We are not overly concerned with adherence to the exacting demands of God. We are complacent, laid-back, thoroughly convinced that an indulgent God loves us no matter what. Voltaire glibly spoke for many of us when he said, "God will forgive me; that's God's job." We aren't even certain we need forgiveness. Religion for many of us has been reduced to little more than trying to have warm, fuzzy feelings about ourselves and the universe.

But Jesus did not come so we could feel different. Jesus came so we could *be* different. This book attempts to map out what it looks like to be different.

Maybe the time has come for us to comprehend what Bonhoeffer meant by "religionless Christianity"—that we go lighter on purely "religious" jargon and activities, and become solidly a part of what's going on in the world.

A MAP OF WHERE WE'RE GOING

We will begin with the fact that Jesus, too, had hands. Jesus was very much human, a participant in the real world, and so he lures us into a very tangible, practical kind of life. In chapters 1 through 4, we will examine the source of all that Jesus did. With his hands he prayed, unrolled scrolls of scripture, and then taught others. The cruciality of communication, of listening to and sharing with God, cannot be over-stated. In *The Story of My Life*, Helen Keller describes that breakthrough day in 1887 when Anne Sullivan signed the letters w-a-t-e-r while hold-ing seven-year-old Helen's hands under running water behind the well-house:

> Suddenly I felt a misty consciousness as of something forgot-ten—a thrill of returning thought; and somehow the mystery of language was revealed to me. I knew then that "w-a-t-e-r" meant the wonderful cool something that was flowing over my hand. That living word awakened my soul, gave it light, hope, joy, set it free![1]

The way Jesus handled his relationship to God may open up for us a consciousness of that living word and set us free.

In the second part of the book, chapters 5 through 9, we will look closely at what Jesus did, whom he touched, how he healed, fed, and served. Too often our attention is riveted on the miraculous in Jesus' life, those dazzling wonders he performed that we can barely believe, much less do ourselves. But the fact is, Jesus did many things we can and must do. Mother Teresa is a modern example, one I refer to frequently in these pages, of someone who eagerly became the hands of Christ. Many of us respond to Mother Teresa's actions by saying, "Oh, she was amaz-ing; she was such a saint"—thereby distancing and excusing ourselves from what we are perfectly capable of doing. Mother Teresa did not leap tall buildings in a single bound. She did not levitate heavy objects, or even wave a hand and put an end to poverty and disease. She simply lifted a spoon of porridge and fed a child; she wielded a cloth and washed away dirt and blood. Most of us could easily be saints if we are willing to give of ourselves in response to the needs of others.

Then, in chapter 10, we will contemplate what happened to Jesus' hands. At the end of the day, those hands that touched, worked, and taught were cruelly pierced. Jesus knew pain, shame, failure. Yet hidden in the moment of crucifixion is our hope. All of our work, our efforts, our mistakes, our grief are gathered, ennobled, and raised up into God's eternal love. In that transformation our hands become the hands of Christ, a part of something bigger than ourselves, members of what is lasting. This is the hope and challenge with which this book will conclude.

But for now, Christ has no body but yours; no feet and no hands but yours. Yours are the hands of Christ.

LIVING HANDS

And the Word became flesh and lived among us,
. . . full of grace and truth. (John 1:14)

Let us pause to remember that Jesus had hands, real hands, with fingers, a pair of thumbs, knuckles, skin, and eventually calluses. It is moving to contemplate what Mary, the mother of Jesus, witnessed during the first days and weeks of her son's nascent life. Parents are ineluctably drawn to the fingers of infants—so small, so perfect, with a surprisingly firm grasp.

We may imagine that Mary toyed gingerly with her son's fingers, admiring their elasticity and form. He no doubt scratched her face, groping after her familiar visage. Nails had to be trimmed, dirt washed away, scrapes bandaged. Mary and Jesus held hands.

Mary nodded when Jesus began to count. She giggled when they tickled one another in those awesome moments of sheer delight that pass too quickly. No doubt, as Luke described it, "Mary treasured all these words and pondered them in her heart" (Luke 2:19).

With the rest of him, Jesus' hands grew larger, stronger, more nimble. He learned to crack his knuckles, to cast shadows against the stone wall of their Nazareth home by flicker of candle, to wave at a friend.

Joseph apprenticed those young hands in rudimentary carving and manual tasks around the household. Jesus' grip tightened as his strength grew, his hands no longer those of a boy but of a man. The day came when he was called forward to unfurl the scroll at synagogue service.

EXALTING LIFE AND BEING GLAD FOR IT

This reverie is meant to remind us that Jesus was a real, human person, that he was fully and bodily a participant in the physical life we take for granted. In the very first chapter of the Bible, God created the first person, a person just as Jesus and you and I are persons, and pronounced humanity "good" (Gen. 1:31). It *is* good. The flesh, the tangible life we wear and can never step outside of, is good. In fact, human life is so good that God chose to be revealed most fully in the tangible body of a man, with hands. The doctrine of the Incarnation is just this: God has not remained aloof from our real life. There is no eternal chasm between worldly life and God. Our hands, and all they touch and feel and do and hold, are where God meets us.

It was Francis of Assisi who thought up the custom of setting up a manger scene at Christmas. Visiting in the town of Greccio, he asked Giovanni, a nobleman, to bring a crib, with hay, oxen, and ass. Citizens streamed out of the city carrying torches, singing hymns. Snow began to fall. They understood, perhaps for the first time, the humanity of Christ, his infant needs and inconveniences, the beauty of that physical moment. Legend has it that as Francis read from Luke 2, a child miraculously appeared, very much alive and verbal, in the crib!

Just as Francis was moved at the very thought of the humanity of

Jesus, we, too, should celebrate this most stunning of amazements. If our Savior entered into the stuff of creation, perhaps it is to be enjoyed by us as well.

When Jesus was a little boy, did grown-ups bend down to ask, "How old are you?" Between two and five, children today certainly love to raise the appropriate number of digits like a salute, a celebration: "I'm three!" Did Jesus as well? Did he mark the years with pleasure, as most children do? Historians tell us that the celebration of birthdays is a modern phenomenon, with cake, candles, presents, party hats. Yet the impulse to commemorate a birthday is at the very essence of our souls. Henri Nouwen wrote that birthdays "need to be celebrated":

> I think it is more important to celebrate a birthday than a successful exam, a promotion, or a victory. Because to celebrate a birthday means to say to someone: "Thank you for being you." Celebrating a birthday is exalting life and being glad for it. On a birthday we do not say: "Thanks for what you did, or said, or accomplished." No, we say: "Thank you for being born and being among us."
>
> On birthdays we celebrate the present. We do not complain about what happened or speculate about what will happen, but we lift someone up and let everyone say: "We love you."[1]

Jesus had hands, and we are alive, and this life is something to be celebrated, and cherished.

RESURRECTION, NOT IMMORTALITY

Five or six centuries before Jesus' birth, God's prophet stood by the waters of Babylon. The Jews were certain they were cut off, forgotten by God and everybody else that mattered. But there they heard these comforting words:

> Can a woman forget her nursing child,
>> or show no compassion for the child of her womb?
> Even these may forget,
>> yet I will not forget you.
> See, I have inscribed you on the palms of my hands. (Isa. 49:15-16)

In all the stuff of our earthly existence, we are never forgotten by God. God loves us, you and me, the real you and me.

But exactly who, or what, is the real you and me? In our culture we often hear that you have a soul that dwells for a while in your body. Or really, you *are* a soul. That invisible part is the real you. And the real you lives forever, even after the body is dead and gone.

But the Bible tells another story. You are not just a soul. You are body *and* soul, which are really just you, all together. Your body is you. And what happens to your body is never remote, or unimportant. Ask anyone suffering chronic pain, or walking around with cancer. Your self includes your body. That means it matters what you do with your body, what Paul called "a temple of the Holy Spirit" (1 Cor. 6:19).

And your body is of continuing concern to God! The New Testament teaches not the immortality of the soul but the resurrection of the body. Jesus was not just a spiritual presence after that first Easter.

He ate and walked; he was visible and touchable (Luke 24:28-30; John 20:27, 21:12). God's hope for us is not just spiritual, but also somehow physical. We will be raised up, our whole self. Whatever we may suffer bodily in this life is not for naught. It matters to God, and God will finally reconcile even our bodies, even all of creation.

Persons of simple faith may grasp this intuitively. A few years ago I buried a woman who had been trapped in a wheelchair for dozens of years. After I said "Amen" by her graveside, her daughter said, "Momma can walk now." She was right. God did not disregard her mother's frailty and suffering. Rather, she has been healed, fully, and is delighting in the joys of having her legs under her again. Jesus, too, had hands, real hands, at his birth, at his death, and even after his resurrection. Our bodies matter. Ultimately, there is redemption for what goes on with our bodies. We are our bodies. Our life, even our eternal life, is inextricably tied up with the real, tangible world.

Little wonder Jesus told us to observe the simple meal we call the Lord's Supper. The Eucharist appeals to all our senses: the feel of the minister's hand, the smell of the bread, the taste of the cup, the sound of prayers for all God's people, the sight of worshipers receiving in humility. Saint Augustine said the sacraments are "visible words." Our life with God was never meant to be mere words but embodied in all that is visible, tangible, real.

TAKING CARE OF GOD'S WORLD

Therefore, this world is the arena of God's activity. "Spiritual" does not mean invisible, but rather that which is animated and motivated and energized by God's living presence. The real world is profoundly spiritual, if we but had the eyes to see. We often need a guide, someone like Annie Dillard, whose books (like *Pilgrim at Tinker Creek* and *Teaching a Stone to Talk*) jostle us into paying attention to the minutiae and grandeur of God's world. This world shouts to us of the incredible lavishness of God's profligacy in nature.

We should notice. And as we notice the complexity and goodness of God's world, we are issued a weighty challenge. Douglas John Hall has shrewdly suggested that the most hopeful metaphor for the church in our milieu is that of "steward."[2] We have often narrowly thought of stewardship as fund-raising with a religious twist. In the Bible, though, a steward is someone the owner trusts to care for his property, a manager who makes crucial decisions in the owner's interests (Luke 12:42-48; 1 Peter 4:7-11). In one of Jesus' most memorable stories, a master gave three servants some talents; the one who protected the money and failed to do anything with it was upbraided (Matt. 25:14-30).

At creation, God charged Adam, Eve, and all humanity with taking care of God's world (Gen. 2:15). Too often, instead of taking care of God's world, we have taken *over* God's world. The explosion of technology in our century has produced a mindset that the world and everything and everyone in it exist for the sake of being exploited, to what end, beyond the making of money, we are never told. It was Thoreau who said that inventions are but improved means to unimproved ends. Our purpose, our reason for being, though, is to take care of God's world, to be faithful stewards of what is God's.

A century ago, evangelists dreamed of "winning" the world for Christ in a generation. Billy Graham has packed stadiums worldwide, and satellites have beamed the Christian message almost everywhere on earth. But the world has not been "won." Far from it. Even in Great Britain and America, home bases for much modern evangelism, church attendance and commitment lag. Perhaps it is time we realize that our calling is not to "win" the world, but rather to care for it. Instead of trying to talk people into thinking as we do, our privilege is simply to love and care for them.

Perhaps in so doing we could even realize that life is in fact good, that it is something we can only receive, like a gift. Many times we live our lives like clenched fists. The clenched fist can do many things: work, hang on to things, impress, frighten, even fight. But, as Frederick Buechner observed in *The Sacred Journey,* "the one thing a clenched fist cannot do is accept, even from *le bon Dieu* [the good God] himself, a helping hand."

A MESSAGE FROM A FAR-OFF LIFE

God extended that helping hand to us in the form of a child, Jesus, with real hands. Wordsworth said,

> A child, more than all other gifts
> That earth can offer to declining man,
> Brings hope with it, and forward-looking thoughts.[3]

Those words echo through the marvelous story of *Silas Marner.* George Eliot told us of this reclusive miser, left utterly wretched and desolate once his stash of money was stolen. But when he came home one evening, he found, instead of "hard coin," some soft curls on his floor— a sleeping child. Eliot magnificently portrays his reaction, a response akin to what we might feel when we contemplate the coming of God into our world as a child.

> He had a dreamy feeling that this child was somehow a message come to him from that far-off life: it stirred . . . old quiverings of tenderness—old impressions of awe at the presentiment of some Power presiding over his life. . . . [We] older human beings, with our inward turmoil, feel a certain awe in the presence of a little child, such as we feel before some quiet majesty or beauty in the earth or sky.

Marner took the little girl on his lap, "trembling with an emotion mysterious to himself, at something unknown dawning on his life. . . . He could only have said that the child was come instead of the gold—that the gold had turned into the child." This child, whom he named Eppie, loved sunshine, sounds, and every other thing in God's world.

> The gold had asked that he should sit weaving longer and longer, deafened to all things except the monotony of his loom; . . . but Eppie called him away from his weaving, and made him think all its pauses a holiday, reawakening his senses with her fresh life, . . . and warming him into joy because *she* had joy.

The hands of Jesus, gifts of joy, the presentiment of some power, a message from a far-off life.

LIVING HANDS

I was blessed to enjoy a wonderful friendship with a retired Baptist minister named Claude Broach. Claude was the kind of friend we all need: wise, experienced, and compassionate, ready to listen and offer a godly perspective. After cancer was diagnosed in his liver, he did his dying quickly and nobly. Just before he died, I asked how it was for him: having ushered hundreds of his church members through their last moments, what was he thinking and feeling in his final days? His answer was twofold: "Well, I am curious." After the word *curious* lingered in the room for a minute, he added: "Mostly, I am focused on the person of Jesus. All the theology I've read, all the talk about denominations and church structures—that's all a blur now. It's the person, Jesus."

It seems to me this should be the focus for all of us, and long before we have been diagnosed with a terminal illness. The person, Jesus. How do we live if our minds are fixed on Jesus? Especially his hands. Yours are the living hands of Christ.

PRAYING HANDS

*In the morning, while it was still very dark, he got up and went out
to a deserted place, and there he prayed. (Mark 1:35)*

There is no shortage of books on the life of prayer and spirituality. Bookstores provide ample space for authors who map out easy steps to a relationship with God, authors who tantalize us with claims of awesome, direct encounters with God, authors who know in astonishing detail what goes on in the realm of angels, authors who portray prayer as a panacea for all life's troubles, the ultimate cure-all for an ailing psyche.

But prayer is hard, a struggle, a genuine grappling with the self, straining out into what feels like darkness, pupils enlarged. Perhaps the steady stream of warm, fuzzy books touting easy connection with God actually masks our deep, aching sense of feeling lost in the universe, so lonely that we will grab onto anything to end our drifting.

LORD, TEACH US TO PRAY

Jesus' hands were praying hands. It is fascinating to reflect upon the role hands play in the way diverse people pray: hands lifted to the skies, as if reaching up to touch, or to be grasped and lifted. Hands folded, reverential, almost wringing with the worries of the world. Hands with palms upturned, as if a receptacle for some morsel, or a drink of water. Hands even clapping in praise and celebration.

Jesus prayed. He withdrew from the crowds to lonely places to be alone with God. Surely, being the Messiah, he had plenty to do! But he prayed. His prayer was evidently of such intimacy that those who lived with him asked for his secret: "Lord, teach us to pray" (Luke 11:1).

Jesus prayed in a quieter era. There were no CDs playing, no factories humming, no traffic. Skies were darker then, the stars brighter. Jesus could feel the immensity of the Milky Way blanketed above him. My children, growing up in artificially luminous cities, have only read about it in their science books.

And Jesus was reared among people who knew how to pray. They recited the *Shema* (Deut. 6:4-9), the age-old reminder to love God and keep God's presence ever before them, at sunrise and at sunset. Jews in Jesus' day prayed morning, afternoon, and evening. Psalms and other recitations filled young minds. Prayer was a normal part of daily life, utterly familiar, embedded in the fiber of being.

The prayers of Jesus were remarkably God-centered. Too often our praying is about *me*. As Dietrich Bonhoeffer wrote while he was in a Nazi concentration camp, weeks before being executed at Flossenbürg for plotting to overthrow Hitler, the Christian life is "not in the first place thinking about one's own needs, problems, sins, and fears, but allowing oneself to be caught up into the way of Jesus Christ."[1]

Prayer is an utterly practical matter. You need a place, a way to ensure quiet, a posture that is relaxed but not lazy, a Bible, an icon or some evocative image like a crucifix, and most importantly, time. Time is a matter of discipline. Even a spiritual giant like Henri Nouwen confessed how readily he let prayer time get squeezed out of his day until his spiritual director advised him to set an inviolable time for it. Leave a meeting or a party; do anything to observe that time, Nouwen's friend encouraged. Make it your most important task; let others know it cannot be changed. At first this will be difficult. But as we are faithful to this discipline, the director affirmed, we are eventually freed from other worries during that time, and it becomes gradually easier to sit quietly in God's presence.[2]

Your body itself will rebel mightily against this very effort. We actually get addicted to stress. The body produces adrenaline to cope with it. But as our stress is prolonged, the body habitually produces a rush of adrenaline. Then, when we even try to slow down, to get quiet, or to pray, our systems, habituated to stress, respond as if something is terribly wrong. The result is a frantically restless mind that cannot focus, a physical urge to get up and do *something*. Or we crumble in utter exhaustion. To make prayer a part of life requires discipline, almost the same kind of rigor demanded of a recovering alcoholic or drug addict. Prayer requires intense, physical practice.

DOES PRAYER WORK?

No matter how accomplished we may become at praying, we may still scratch our heads and wonder: *Does prayer work?* In a day of particle physics and genetics, who in his right mind could believe that muttering wishes skyward can alter the course of events? Of course, there are countless stories of answered prayer. Cancer mysteriously vanishes from someone's body. A needed sum of money appears, without explanation, at exactly the right time. An "accidental" meeting results in marriage. Circumstances far too quirky to qualify as mere luck conspire for a happy ending.

Now there are even published studies indicating that prayer works. Not just peace of mind, but even longevity and recovery from disease are linked to the practice of prayer. The *Southern Medical Journal* reported that, over a ten-month period, prayed-for coronary patients got well more quickly than the control (unprayed-for) group, who required more ventilatory assistance, antibiotics, and diuretics.[3] Prayer must work after all—although I think if I were in that control group, I'd sue the pious for negligence.

In a sense, stories of answered prayer are thrilling, encouraging, and hopeful. Yet often I let out a sigh of despair when I hear a miraculous story or read a study about answered prayer. Even if God dashes off a miracle now and then, most of the time, if we are really honest, prayer just doesn't work at all. Haven't you pleaded with God for the recovery of a loved one, only to have those prayers seem to fall harmlessly to the floor? Who believes that God answers only the superholy, or those who pray more minutes, or in greater numbers, or with more fervor, or utilizing the proper formulas? If prayer works, it doesn't seem to work very efficiently, or frequently.

Perhaps we need to reexamine this whole business of praying *for* this or that. Prayer's value for Jesus did not rise or fall depending on whether it "worked" or not. He prayed in Gethsemane to avoid death! For Jesus, prayer was about love, not consequences. His relationship with God, whom he called "Abba," an unusually affectionate word, was so passionate that the two of them had to be together regularly.

Prayer is actually an end in itself because it is communion with

God. That same God is full of compassion, gravely concerned about the troubles of the world. Prayer calls us into communion, not only with God, but with all God loves. Therefore, prayer, practiced even amateurishly, catapults us out into the streets to be in service.

THE ANSWER TO SOMEBODY'S PRAYER

A major problem with stories of answered prayer is that they can lead us so easily to slump into passivity. We pray and we wait, and wait, for some thunderous response from the heavens, when perhaps the answer to prayer is literally at our own fingertips.

Several years ago, several churches in our community brought Millard Fuller to Charlotte. Millard Fuller was a wealthy businessman who heard God's calling and started Habitat for Humanity, a ministry of building affordable housing for the working poor. (Jesus, apprenticed as a carpenter, must take special delight in Habitat!) We decided that instead of having a minister or some other professional introduce Fuller, we would invite a resident from a Habitat house. So we asked Melissa Cornett—a tall, gangly woman, not an accomplished speaker. She was nervous. She poked around for words but then suddenly began to speak to Fuller, who was sitting on the front row.

"Millard Fuller, you are the answer to my prayer. I grew up in a tenement, a terrible place, full of drugs, violence. I was nobody, knew I'd always be nobody. I had a little boy—and there he was, in a terrible place, full of drugs, violence. I knew he'd never be anybody either. So I got on my knees and I prayed. I prayed hard. I said, 'Lord, I will do anything; I will give up my life. But please, please, I just want my boy to have a chance to be somebody.'

"Millard Fuller, when God told you to give away your money, you were the answer to my prayer. I heard about Habitat, and I got to build a house. I met President Jimmy Carter. We got a house, a nice house.

"Before we moved in, my boy had started school, but his teacher said he was slow and he would probably never catch up. He never smiled. But then we moved into our new house. He had his own room. And he began to shine that day. He got to where he played and had fun. And he started making good grades in school. Now he's in the third grade, and he's making straight A's. The other day, my boy said to me, 'Momma, do you know what I want to be when I grow up?' I said, 'No, what do you want to be?' He said, 'I'm going to be a doctor.'

"Millard Fuller, you're the answer to my prayer."

About this time, Melissa figured she had talked too long and gotten off track—so, a little embarrassed, she said, "Well, without any further ado, here's Millard Fuller."

Now, if you've ever been part of a standing ovation, you know how it goes: one person rises, then another, finally everyone else. But once in awhile, an entire body of people leap to their feet. That's what they did for this wonderful woman's speech. Melissa walked off to the side and turned to clap for Millard Fuller. I put my arm around her, pointed to the crowd, and said, "Look, Melissa. They're not clapping for him. They're clapping for you."

Can you imagine anything better than discovering one day you were the answer to somebody's prayer?

BIG ASSIGNMENTS

In the last lectures he gave before his death in 1968, Karl Barth described prayer as an uprising against the disorder of the world. Ultimately, prayer isn't about me and my problems. Prayer is getting swept up into something larger, into the movement of God's way in the world. Elie Wiesel once said that if an angel says, "Be not afraid," you'd better watch out: a big assignment is on the way! Prayer is discerning and welcoming big assignments from God.

Maybe those journalists who study prayer ought to study what happens when people pray in the sense of accepting big assignments, when we discern our call to be part of an uprising, to use what God has given us to change what needs changing. But we know what the results of the study would be. Talk about the power of prayer! The problem is, most of us keep volunteering to be in the control group.

Prayer is an act of yielding control, the acceptance of a mission. What Archbishop Oscar Romero said about worship applies to all forms of prayer:

When we leave Mass,
we ought to go out
the way Moses descended Mount Sinai:
    with his face shining,
    with his heart brave and strong,
        to face the world's difficulties.[4]

Certainly the world will be difficult. Jesus learned this all too well as a result of his most poignant moment of prayer. In Gethsemane, Jesus poured out his heart to God and learned that prayer is not a tool to get things under control, that prayer does not always ease our burdens. Prayer is rather when we yield everything to God, when we can say, "Into your hands I commit my spirit," when we orient ourselves to the inscrutable ways of God in the world, no matter the cost.

PRAYING HANDS

In whatever manner you are most comfortable, or perhaps even experimenting a bit, fold or lift or open your hands in prayer. Don't be in a hurry. Picture Jesus at prayer. Relax your hands, as if letting go of your grip on your life. Be caught up into the way of Jesus Christ. Don't be afraid. Even now, a big assignment is finding its way into your hands. It is heavy, but it feels right. It fits. And it matters. It is the answer to somebody's prayer.

Yours are the praying hands of Christ.

UNFURLING HANDS

He went to the synagogue. . . .He stood up to read,
and the scroll of the prophet Isaiah was given to him.
He unrolled the scroll. (Luke 4:16-17)

Back in 1947, a Ta'amireh tribesman was pitching stones into a cave. Something shattered inside. His friend squeezed through a crevice and found some old jars, most of them empty. But inside one jar they found some scrolls. After finagling that involved an antiquities dealer named Kando in Bethlehem, the Metropolitan (leader of the Syrian-Jacobite Church) in Jerusalem, and several scholars—not to mention some sticky political maneuvering—some of these now-famous Dead Sea Scrolls eventually came to rest in the Shrine of the Book at the Israel Museum. The most spectacular find proved to be an intact, complete scroll containing the entire Book of Isaiah, dated to just before the time of Christ.

With his hands, Jesus unfurled scrolls, including an Isaiah scroll, very much like the one found near the Dead Sea, and read aloud. Luke 4:16-30 relates an unforgettable incident. The synagogue service that day was normal enough. Psalms were sung, the *Shema* ("Hear O Israel, the Lord our God is one Lord") was recited, and the usual eighteen benedictions were pronounced. The presiding officer invited a young man, home from an extended journey, to serve as the reader for the day. Jesus unrolled the Isaiah parchment and began,

> The Spirit of the Lord is upon me,
>> because he has anointed me
>>> to bring good news to the poor.
> He has sent me to proclaim release to the captives
>> and recovery of sight to the blind.

When Jesus was done he handed the scroll back to the attendant and sat down. Their gazes fixed on him, his townspeople were stunned and appalled when he said, "Today this scripture has been fulfilled in your hearing." In a frenzied rage they nearly threw him off a cliff.

TAKING THE BIBLE LITERALLY

Jesus took the Bible literally—but he wasn't a fundamentalist. He never pointed to the "facts" of the Bible and claimed scientific truth for them. No, Jesus took the Bible literally in the same way Saint Francis of Assisi took it literally: he thought he was supposed to *do* what it said!

In the year 1209, Francis went to one of Assisi's great churches, San Nicolo, and asked the priest to open the Bible at random. Three times the priest did so, reading to Francis these words: "If you wish to be perfect, go, sell your possessions, and give the money to the poor" (Matt. 19:21). He closed the book in silence, then reopened it and read, "Take no bag for your journey" (Luke 10:4). And then the third word: "If any want to become my followers, let them deny themselves" (Matt. 16:24).

Francis did just that. And other young men—Bernard, Peter, Giles,

Leo—did likewise. The elders of the city were in such consternation that they locked up the apparently crazed young men in quarantine, believing some sort of bizarre contagion was on the loose that might unravel the fabric of the region's economic life.

Jesus "performed" the ancient scriptures with faithfulness, but also with creativity. And while he was acting out the scriptures, he was at the same time creating scripture himself—without putting one drop of ink onto any scroll! Jesus' words, Jesus' actions—they were the stuff of memory that would shape the church for the balance of its life. Jesus told stories, not so they would rest idly in some treasury of religious memory, but so they would stretch the imagination and then take on flesh in real life.

His stories obviously are not true in the literal sense. In *The Life of Brian,* a Monty Python film, Brian pretends to be a wise teacher, and begins a story: "A man had two sons." An onlooker chides Brian for not knowing the names of the two sons, angrily concluding, "He's making it up." When Jesus began, "A man had two sons" (Luke 15:11), he *was* making it up—just as he was when he told the one about the sower who threw seed all over the road, thorns, and rocks. Jesus didn't observe a crazed sower. He made the story up. Quite a few stories in the Bible have every telltale sign that they were intended to be heard as made-up, as once-upon-a-time kinds of legends.

Mind you, this doesn't make them less true. If anything they are more true by virtue of not being literal reports about what one individual did. A man had two sons. One squandered his living in a strange land; the other stayed home and felt smug about it. What could be more true, not just about a man with a name and address, but about every man?

THE HOLEY BIBLE

In the Bible we read the words of people who knew God, who were intimately acquainted with those defining moments in the young life of God's people. For the first Christians, the Bible was not some household icon with an expensive cover to be waved or even just read. The stories of the Bible were a springboard for action, for shaping how they thought and what they were busy with all day long. The Bible was there for the doing.

Nothing is easy about this doing of scripture. Mark Twain once said that he was most bothered not by the parts of the Bible he couldn't understand, but by the parts he could understand. Jim Wallis tells about meeting with seminary students in Chicago. They took scissors to a Bible and physically excised every passage that speaks about the poor. Gradually, major portions of the prophets, the Psalms, laws in Leviticus, the teachings of Jesus, and the epistles were snipped and clipped until the Bible was in shreds. Wallis called the result that "holey Bible."[1]

Aren't we guilty of such a selective, piecemeal reading of the Bible? And when we pick and choose passages we are fond of, isn't this really an evasion of God's claim on us, yet at the same time a superficial stab at pretending we are in sync with God's ways?

The Bible exists to be put into practice. "Be doers of the word, and not merely hearers" (James 1:22). In fact, as long as we approach Bible passages merely intellectually, we never fully understand them. Saint Athanasius, a bishop from the fourth century, put it best:

For the searching and right understanding of the Scriptures there is need of a good life and a pure soul, and for Christian virtue to guide the mind to grasp, so far as human nature can, the truth concerning God the Word. One cannot possibly understand the teaching of the saints unless one has a pure mind and is trying to imitate their life. . . . Anyone who wishes to understand the mind of the sacred writers must first cleanse his own life, and approach the saints by copying their deeds.[2]

CORRECTIVE LENSES

Many Christians handle the Bible as if it were a Ouija board or an answer book, chock-full of orders and commands from on high. But as you read the Bible, you find stories: earthy, humorous, even bizarre stories. There is love poetry, and there are plenty of songs; there are pithy little sayings and some longer sermons. We see people trying to figure God out and struggling to get along with their neighbors. God didn't dictate every word, or drop it down from a cloud. The process was more elusive, and more real. The results are imperfect, yet more than good enough. The pictures, colors, and shapes of the Bible, if we look carefully enough, are the greatest images we have in our exploration of God.

What all those stories and pictures and colors and shapes add up to is something like a great mural. Up close you see various details. From a distance you see the big picture—an inviting image of life in the world with God. Instead of an answer book, the Bible is more like a good pair of corrective lenses: we have this astigmatism, spiritually speaking, and the Bible corrects our vision, focusing our eyes.

We might also think of it like this: the Bible portrays a different paradigm for how to view reality. When Nicolaus Copernicus first suggested that the earth was not located at the center of the universe, critics scoffed. But he had done a lot of looking up, at the stars, the planets, the moon, and he had figured out the earth was circling the sun. Once other watchers began looking at the skies from that perspective, more of what they saw made sense. Previously unexplained phenomena now fit neatly into the Copernican scheme.

Perhaps when we step into the world of the Bible it will be for us like Copernicus's discovery. The biblical writers did a lot of looking up, or looking within. They contemplated what they had seen and heard in such depth that they began to understand the underlying order of things. And they couldn't keep it to themselves. They wrote it down, so we, too, could look up and within and understand a deeper dimension of reality than is obvious to our normal senses. Previously unexplained phenomena in our lives now make sense as part of God's larger purpose.

Truth is not something you figure out today for yourself. Truth precedes all of us and claims us. Truth perseveres; it has some antiquity about it. Admittedly, in our culture this idea will strike many as humorous. But as John Updike put it, "Laugh at ministers all you want, they have the words we need to hear, the ones the dead have spoken."[3] Laugh if you will, but we highly educated, modern people may prove to be the real laughingstock. My grandparents could be perfectly described by these words from Allan Bloom's *The Closing of the American Mind:*

> My grandparents were ignorant people by our standards, and my grandfather held only lowly jobs. But their home was spiritually rich because all the things done in it . . . found their origin in the Bible's commandments, and their explanation in the Bible's stories. . . . I do not believe that my generation, my

cousins who have been educated in the American way, all of whom are M.D.s or Ph.D.s, have any comparable learning. When they talk, about heaven and earth, the relations between men and women, parents and children, the human condition, I hear nothing but cliches, superficialities, the material of satire.[4]

We must put on these corrective lenses of the Bible, as often our forebears did, to see God and to see the world we are called to love and serve.

UNFURLING THE WORLD

To interpret the Bible rightly we need to read the world every bit as carefully and accurately as we read the Bible itself. The temptation to turn our heads and disregard the world is potent. To contemplate the face of poverty, the proliferation of drugs, the vacuum where morality ought to be, the plight of children, and the malaise of cynicism—it is far less painful just to stick our heads in the sand, to rush off after every diversion.

But Jesus read his world, diagnosing his culture deftly. It is said that Karl Barth climbed into the pulpit with the Bible under one arm, the newspaper under the other. Finding the intersection between the Bible and the real world is no easy matter. If we misconstrue what is going on in the world, we will never apply the Bible properly. We will wind up with nothing to offer the world but irrelevant moralisms and tired platitudes.

Who is reading the Bible, and where, and when, make all the difference. For example, in the comfortable but confused milieu of the American middle class, the words of Psalm 130—"Out of the depths I cry to you"—remind us of the depths of depression or anxiety. But if you read the same psalm in the turmoil of Third World political oppression, "the depths" may be construed as a prison cell or the aftermath of a street shooting. We need to remember where we read the Bible, but also where others are reading it.

It is sobering to contemplate what the poor of the world are coping with—and to develop a sense of solidarity with them. All the places, you see, are connected. We may focus only on our backyard, but God cares about the whole world, all its people. It is the height of foolishness for passengers on the upper deck to gaze below and say, "Your part of the ship is sinking." God put us in this boat together.

Timing is everything. Plenty of preachers wave a floppy Bible at people, shouting, "Sinners, repent!" In the Middle Ages, or maybe just a generation ago, people were burdened with a keen sense of guilt, an awareness that offenses large and small were piling up every moment, and that a righteous God might strike them down. But nowadays, many people do not really know enough about God's law to comprehend that they have violated it. According to Douglas John Hall, their problem is not so much that they are like Prometheus, rebellious violator of divine decrees. Rather, they are like Sisyphus, simply exhausted and worn out by trying to hoist their troubles on their own shoulders, pushing valiantly up a mountain, only to have the burden roll down on top of them again. We had better know where people are before we push the Bible up against them.

We need to grapple with the big, systemic causes of dysfunction in our society—how we distribute justice, how our individual greed and consumption make us numb, how racial attitudes and public policies adversely affect those who hurt the most. But simultaneously we must remember to engage daily in those tangible, heroic deeds that seem small yet are very doable: volunteering, delivering a meal, reading to a child.

Mother Teresa was once invited to an international hunger conference in Bombay. Having lost her way, arriving late, the meeting already begun, she found a starving man on the steps outside. Inside they were analyzing trends and statistics; outside, she picked the man up and fed him. Like Jesus, we have to notice, to get up, to do something.

UNFURLING THE FUTURE

The first time I ever preached in an African-American church, I grew nervous as the enthusiasm of the prayers and singing surged. Finally, the host pastor urged me into the pulpit by saying, "Come now, Brother Howell, unfurl for us the scroll of heaven, that we might hear the angels sing." This made me really nervous.

But this notion of unfurling the scroll of heaven is crucial. By "heaven" I mean the future, God's eternal future, the way things ultimately are meant to be. Martin Luther King Jr., in his last Sunday morning sermon, said, "The arc of a moral universe is long, but it bends toward justice."[5] Jesus taught his disciples to pray by saying, "Your will be done, on earth as it is in heaven." That is, if we can contemplate now how things will be, in God's good time, then we know better how to act in the present, what to strive after, which priorities are worth the while.

This attitude is hope. Hope differs from optimism. The optimistic believe it will be sunny this afternoon, that we will at any moment get our act together and solve our problems. Late in his life, a tired Martin Luther King shared with his old Dexter Avenue Baptist Church that although he still had hope, he was no longer optimistic. Hope depends not entirely on us, but on God.

Justice will dawn. But maybe not tomorrow. Changing the world is not something you can scribble down on next Thursday's to-do list. And on your first lunge at a problem you will likely fall flat on your face. But hope can withstand failure; it can cope with disappointment. Hope is committed to doing what is good, what is right, quite apart from whether or not the effort meets with success.

Hope demands that we notice our world, and that we take responsibility for it and for each other. Saint Augustine suggested poetically that hope has two beautiful daughters: *anger* at the way things are, and *courage* to see to it they do not remain the way they are. It is a healthy thing to get angry, to be outraged—and then to get busy working for something just because it is good and needed. With courage we embrace a very long-term task with energy and patience. As Reinhold Niebuhr said, "Nothing that is worth doing can be achieved in our lifetime."

UNFURLING HANDS

Picture Jesus unrolling that Isaiah scroll. At an angle to that unfurled parchment, imagine a large map of the world, still curled up at the edges, but spread out. Then envision the space just above and below the scroll and the map somehow pulled back, catching both them and you up into a broad space, inclined upward.

Listen. And look. See what is revealed at this still point, in this pregnant pause between the word and our world, between time and eternity. Then go with it. Yours are the hands of Christ.

TEACHING HANDS

They were astounded at his teaching,
for he taught them as one having authority. (Mark 1:22)

When Jesus taught, did he use his hands? We know where Jesus taught. He could deploy a fishing boat as his pulpit, taking advantage of little curvatures in the hillside above the shore only a few feet away, listeners sitting on the grass as in a theater. What gestures did he make as he spoke? An intense wave, a gentle beckoning, a fist clenched, a palm cupped?

Surely he used a finger to point: "Look at the birds of the air" or "Consider the lilies" (Matt. 6:26, 28). He could direct the gaze of his listeners to Bethsaida or Korazim or another "city built on a hill" (Matt. 5:14), or to the tombs of the prophets above the Kidron Valley (Matt. 23:27-31). The stuff of his preaching was always nearby: sheep, shepherds, clouds gathering, fields, homes, fig trees.

A SOWER WENT OUT TO SOW

One thing is certain: Jesus spoke about everyday, tangible, utterly familiar things. He never said, "There are five dogmas to which you must give mental assent." In part his style was a strategy to communicate clearly

43

with his listeners who were not tutored in abstract, philosophical modes of thought. But it was also a broad hint that our life with God is lived out not in some ethereal, intellectual realm, but in the mundane material of daily life. A sower going out to sow. A man hiring workers all day long for his vineyard. A woman sweeping the floor in search of a coin. Sewing a patch on clothing, pouring wine into skins. Bridesmaids storing up oil for their torches. A man, beaten and left for dead, bypassed by holy men, helped by a foreigner. Two houses, one built on a solid, stone foundation, the other on sandy soil. Two men going into God's house to pray, one full of confidence, the other meek and humble. Taste this salt! And take a look at this mustard bush! How do you pull weeds in a field without ruining the wheat? You have the chance to buy the world's greatest pearl. And over there is a fig tree—with no figs.

Stories like these expose, shape, change us in ways no enumeration of "points" or beliefs can. Life does not feel like six ideas or seven propositions. Life feels like a story, packed with dramatic turns, the mundane, mere trifles, and mind-boggling surprises. In fact, Jesus usually packed a surprise or two in his stories. That a father had two sons and one frittered away his wealth is normal enough (Luke 15:11-32); but a father running down the road to welcome the prodigal instead of doling out an "I told you so"? A sower casting seeds was an essential feature of the landscape (Mark 4:3-9); but what kind of sower thoughtlessly flung seed on the road or among thorns and rocks? Vineyard workers were always for hire (Matthew 20:1-16); but what kind of business pays the same whether you work all day or just an hour?

Jesus deliberately told stories that might not be entirely self-evident on first hearing. He intended his hearers to listen, reflect, remember, ponder, question, regroup, think again, discuss, get beyond the obvious. "Let anyone with ears listen!" (Matthew 11:15) is an invitation to knead and wrestle with and savor the story, its inexhaustible truth never fully zapped.

And there was this open-endedness about his stories. The prodigal son returns home; the older son grouses outside the party; the father pleads with him to join them. But does he?

Jesus' teaching was never simple logic and verbiage. At the Last Supper, he could have instructed his disciples sternly, "No elbowing to get the best seat!" Instead he simply rose in silence, took up basin, water, and towel, and washed their feet (John 13:5). More eloquent than words.

YOURS IS NOT TO REASON WHY

Perhaps Jesus was also giving us a clue about how to communicate. Too often we wave a Bible at people, telling them in so many words to "take it or leave it." Too many sermons assume listeners know their Bible when increasing numbers either don't own one, or leave this seemingly vague volume to gather dust. When people have searching, honest questions and even doubts about the Bible, we often stupidly counter by saying, "You've just got to have faith!" We expect people to bury their questions, and obey blindly—in the manner of what Tennyson wrote about the Lighthouse Brigade: "Theirs not to reason why, / Theirs but to do and die."[1]

Take it or leave it? No wonder plenty of people leave it. We have to figure out how to connect with people, with their real-life stories, where they are. With open hands we need to gesture toward the familiar, to help people catch a glimpse of the gospel hidden and yet revealed in the everyday. A toddler learns to walk. Rain softens hard ground. Mother and daughter embrace.

Human experience opens a few windows that may surprise us. For instance, you do not have to look hard to find a church person who is swift to condemn homosexuality. And you would not need to look hard to find a homosexual, thoroughly alienated by hateful attitudes in the church, who has with exemplary compassion and tenderness cared for a friend dying of the horror we call AIDS. God's truth, the love of God, is more clearly evidenced in the behavior of the one ostracized from the church than in the smugness of the one convinced of his holiness and rightness.

Literature, too, can tell the truth about God and the Christian life. The apostle Paul tells the truth about how mixed up we are. But read Pat Conroy's novels about dysfunctional families, about how we cannot extricate ourselves from the chains of guilt and evil. The short stories of Flannery O'Connor expose our hypocrisy and hollowness with unmatched eloquence. If we would explore our rootlessness, how our supposedly upward mobility subtly empties our lives of what is substantive, we can read Wallace Stegner's *The Spectator Bird.* If we want to get people thinking about what they are called to in this life, and if there is some underlying purpose to it all, where better to begin than by reading John Irving's *A Prayer for Owen Meany?*

Surprisingly, words may tell even deeper than expected truths. For instance, Ernest Hemingway's *A Farewell to Arms,* a virtual ode to hopelessness, contains the following remarkable sentence: "The world breaks every one and afterward many are strong at the broken places."

TURNED UPSIDE DOWN

In Jesus' teaching, such surprises were normal. When Jesus walked into the villages around the Sea of Galilee, his listeners had a mental map of the world, an orientation from which they viewed their lives: what had value, what to avoid, which direction to go. Jesus turned that map sideways. Or he refolded it and rearranged it. He turned our usual view of reality upside down.

In one of his wonderful interrogations of a would-be student, Socrates cornered Callicles until the hapless victim exclaimed, "If you are serious and what you say is true, then surely the life of us mortals must be turned upside down and apparently we are everywhere doing the opposite of what we should."[2] Or as Paul described it to another group of Greeks, these in Corinth: "God's foolishness is wiser than human wisdom, and God's weakness is stronger than human strength. . . . God chose what is foolish in the world to shame the wise" (1 Cor. 1:25, 27).

Teachers in our public schools may recognize what this is all about. In *Teaching as a Subversive Activity,* Neil Postman and Charles Weingartner make an impressive case that there is a crying need for students to step outside the given parameters and ask hard questions, to cut through the inertia of the status quo, to overturn, at least mentally, our crazed culture.

To be Jesus' students, we have to get the hang of this inverted perspective. Literary critics in recent decades have evolved what they call a "hermeneutics of suspicion," where we look at everything written or said with a questioning eye, living on the lookout for veiled motives and bogus or self-interested priorities. We never stifle questions. Nothing gives birth to deepened understanding like a good question, and even a healthy dosage of doubt, that alleged enemy of faith. Mark Helprin wrote, "All great discoveries . . . are products as much of doubt as of certainty, and the two in opposition clear the air for marvelous accidents."[3]

When we look out at the world and at the usual wisdom of the day, we should at least cock our heads a little and reconsider things from the curious perspective of the teacher Jesus. This teacher spoke admiringly of a sower who threw seed among thorns. He extolled a man who paid his one-hour workers the same as those who had sweated all day. This teacher did not wish to be honored for his great instruction with accolades, laurels, or gold, but preferred a shameful, excruciating death as recompense for his words. This teacher likely nodded when a wise person said, "You shall know the truth, and the truth shall make you odd."

In the end, Jesus taught not by his words or even by his life, but by his death. The all-encompassing lesson in the curriculum was the awesome love of God, too profound for mere words. Jesus suffered and was crucified to give us the clearest even if oblique glimpse of the extent of God's love for us.

TEACHING HANDS

Leading a retreat in 1928, Evelyn Underhill said, "The members of Christ are the lips through which He speaks, the eyes through which He looks into ours, the hands reaching out for the gifts we are supposed to be so glad to offer Him."[4] How can we be the lips of Christ? How can we communicate who Christ was, and is, in a manner that carries conviction and at the same time is open and respectful of listeners who disagree or do not yet believe?

Whatever we may say, may we remember that the lesson those around us will pick up on most accurately will be our lives. At a certain point, words fail us. We are subjected to just too many of them in our media-blitzed society. And, after all, we are talking about something elusive, the presence of God in real, human life.

When the church canonized Saint Clare, the young woman who was the friend and spiritual companion of Saint Francis in Assisi, her dossier read, "Her very life was for others a school of instruction and doctrine. In this book of life others learned the rule of life; in this mirror of life the others beheld the path of their own life."[5]

Hers were the teaching hands of Christ. Yours are the teaching hands of Christ.

TOUCHING HANDS

Moved with pity,
Jesus stretched out his hand and
touched him. (Mark 1:41)

We cannot think very long about the hands of Jesus without marveling over all the people that he simply touched. He took children in his arms (Mark 10:16), laid hands on them and blessed them. Often when he healed, he took the person by the hand and led him somewhere (Mark 8:23). He grasped the hand of a panicked Peter, who was sinking into the Sea of Galilee (Matt. 14:31). He gently cleansed the feet of his disciples (John 13:5).

Beyond question, one of the reasons Jesus was eventually put to death was that he touched all the wrong people. He could have healed those ostracized, untouchable lepers at a distance. But he disregarded all warnings and overcame their isolation and touched them. His very religious critics complained that "he eats with sinners" (Luke 15:2). Among his friends were despised tax collectors, a Samaritan woman, the demon-possessed—all the people everyone had seemingly good reason to avoid. Even harlots were included in his embrace.

Jesus understood that we are all kin, that beneath all the superficial stuff that we latch onto (and which cause division and a bogus sense of superiority), the same blood flows through all our veins. We all hurt, hope, dream, weep.

THE CONTENTS OF THEIR CHARACTER

At the safe distance of a couple of thousand years, touching the untouchable seems pretty innocuous. In our culture, touching people, especially those who are different, can create anxiety and fear. Just when we are becoming aware of the startling diversity of people in our world, we are losing our ability to connect with people who are different.

On August 28, 1963, Martin Luther King Jr. stood before hundreds of thousands of people clustered in front of the Lincoln Memorial. His sermon started poorly. But Mahalia Jackson, sitting behind him on the rostrum, urged him on: "Tell 'em about the dream." In a moment forever etched in our society's memory, King forsook his written manuscript and soared higher than the heavens, taking us along for the ride, as in a chariot of heavenly fire.

I still have a dream. . . .

I have a dream that one day on the red hills of Georgia sons of former slaves and sons of former slaveowners will be able to sit down together at the table of brotherhood. . . .

I have a dream that my four little children will one day live in a nation where they will not be judged by the color of their skin but by the content of their character. . . .

I have a dream that one day, the state of Alabama, . . . will be transformed into a situation where little black boys and black girls will be able to join hands with little white boys and little white girls as sisters and brothers.[1]

Mahalia Jackson was celebrating, saying, "My Lord! My Lord!" After letting freedom ring from the Alleghenies to the Rockies to Stone Mountain, King finished with a flurry:

> And when *this* happens . . . we will be able to speed up that day when all of God's children, black men and white men, Jews and Gentiles, Protestants and Catholics, will be able to join hands and sing in the words of the old Negro spiritual, "Free at last! Free at last! Thank God almighty, we are free at last!"[2]

King's words always send a chill along my spine. But an entire generation later, the chill feels cold, more like a shudder, for we have been unable to speed up that day. We are not free. We rarely sit together at the table.

I keep encountering folks—good, sensitive, intelligent, progressive folks—who were idealistic, as I was, in the sixties, only to be hit with round after round of disappointment. In response, they've given up, like the woman in Alice Walker's novel *The Temple of My Familiar.* Once a whirling dervish of doing good around her church, she gave up, sat down, and just stared out her back window for three years: "She gave up trying to improve the world and, instead, declined to notice it."

But when anyone gives up, we all lose. There is some invisible interconnection between people that suggests that if one person is diminished we are all diminished. My joy is less than it could be because of the misery of someone I don't even know. Logic screams out against such a thought, but it is the way God has wired the universe. In his last Sunday morning sermon, at the National Cathedral in Washington, King said, "For some strange reason I can never be what I ought to be until you are what you ought to be. And you can never be what you ought to be until I am what I ought to be."[3]

HOW TO DISAGREE

Our divisions are not restricted to race. Almost any difference can become a source of division. We certainly have forgotten how to disagree with each other. One of the treasures of a democracy should be that we can disagree without having to go out and shoot the other person. But when someone thinks other thoughts, we rush off and try to find a little clump of people who agree with ourselves, or look like us.

This habit becomes especially ugly when we try to attach God to our small-minded attitudes. There are always those theological sadists who proclaim that AIDS is God's judgment on homosexuals. We might as well say that heart disease is God's vengeance on those who indulge in a high-cholesterol diet, or that the common cold is holy retribution on those who go out-of-doors. It is staggering to contemplate the ways we shut out and pass judgment on people because of what we think they have done, yet never questioning our own foibles, or what we are called to do for others.

We lunge toward the slightest opportunity to stack people one on top of another—and to place ourselves as high up as possible. Scrooge's nephew would remind us of one of the lessons learned from Christ's birth:

Christmas-time . . . is the only time I know of, in the long cal-
endar of the year, when men and women seem by one consent
to open their shut-up hearts freely, and to think of people below
them as if they really were fellow-passengers to the grave, and
not another race of creatures bound on other journeys.[4]

Even among denominations, and certainly within denominations,
we find ways to build fences over which no one can or wants to reach
to touch those on the other side. The Lord's Supper, that greatest of
earthly gifts Jesus gave us, has been transformed from an invitation into
a test of orthodoxy, from a feast for everyone into an exclusive supper
club. Today theology is not so much the glorification of God as it is a
competition among authors and denominations.

WAITING TOGETHER

Increasingly we need to learn how to touch persons of other faiths.
Once upon a time, people in most parts of America could imagine that
everybody was at least nominally Christian. But now, in every region,
there are Muslims, Buddhists, Jews, and many more. Can we learn what
Mother Teresa meant when she said, "I love all religions, but I am in
love with my own religion"?

My friend Jim Bennett, the rabbi at Temple Beth El in Charlotte,
took a stab at a children's sermon one Sabbath. He asked, "Who can tell
me the name of somebody in the Bible?"

The first child spoke up: "God!"

"Well, good answer, even though we can't see God, that's fine.
Name another character."

Loud as could be, a little boy chimed in: "Jesus!"

"Well, good. Jesus, you know, is in the Bible the Christians read, but he isn't in our Bible." Holding his breath, he told me later, he imagined the next answer might just be "Mary!"

Jews and Christians don't believe all the same things. We may certainly be friends, and we certainly respect and listen to each other. But Hanukkah isn't the "Jewish Christmas." And perhaps when Christians talk about Jesus being the fulfillment of the Old Testament, the promised one, we should do so with utter humility, cognizant that we have friends and neighbors who believe differently. It was not all that long ago that Christians, claiming complete knowledge about the Scriptures, led their Jewish neighbors into concentration camps and killed millions of them. Even today, Jewish children are at times pressured by public schoolteachers to take tests or play in the band or practice some sport on Jewish holy days.

Maybe we should contemplate this wonderful thought from the great Jewish writer Martin Buber, who told a group of Christian priests:

> What is the difference between Jews and Christians? We all await the Messiah. You believe He has already come and gone, while we do not. I therefore propose that we await Him together. And when He appears, we can ask Him: "Were you here before?". . . And I hope that at that moment I will be close enough to whisper in his ear, "For the love of heaven, don't answer."[5]

PRACTICING TOUCH

How do we begin to touch as Jesus touched? I knew a man in college who was painfully shy and found it difficult even to shake hands. A wise counselor advised him to exploit his active imagination, picturing himself slapping buddies on the back, hugging friends, tugging on the fingers of a toddler. And he was also told to practice on some safe people— like me. It was awkward at first. The effort required of my friend much patience, time, and the ability to wait for a long-held mentality to change. But he did change, and to this day he is known as an extremely warm, affectionate man.

We also must recognize that some people wear an overlay of distrust. Old wounds fester between people. Friends, relatives, and particularly married couples who have dealt with betrayal know that trust is not restored when one person blurts out, "Trust me!" Rather, thousands of little trustworthy acts, performed over weeks and months, rebuild that fragile treasure in our souls called trust.

We need to apply all our creativity in reaching out to others. Go out of your normal way to see and encounter others who are different. John 4 tells us that Jesus *had* to go through Samaria—not the usual or safest route. But he had to go there, to touch someone, specifically the woman at the well. Jesus *had* to go there to knock down one more fence.

Today we can do the same thing. Churches can establish worship experiences with other congregations. We can reach out: a man in my city urged a half million people to go to lunch on Tuesdays with someone of another race. Probably a couple of hundred did. Small glimpses of the touching hands of Christ.

HOW SAFELY I AM HELD

Mostly we need to see others with the eyes of Christ. Dostoevsky said that to love another person is to see that person as God intended him to be. We are all sinners. We have all been wounded. We all have hopes and dreams. Above all else in life, we all need to know the love and mercy of God. Henri Nouwen wrote a beautiful book in 1992 called *The Return of the Prodigal Son*. It is a sustained reflection upon what Rembrandt did with Jesus' story in Luke 15. The painting, which hangs in The Hermitage in St. Petersburg, portrays an aged, nearly blind father embracing his ragged son come home. The left hand is strong, muscular. The right hand is soft, tender, like a mother's hand. The light is focused on those hands, which Nouwen describes:

> In them mercy becomes flesh; upon them forgiveness, recon-
> ciliation, and healing come together, and, through them, not
> only the tired son, but also the worn-out father find their rest.
> From the moment I first saw [the painting], I felt drawn to
> those hands. I did not fully understand why. But gradually
> over the years I have come to know those hands. They have
> held me from the hour of my conception, they welcomed me
> at my birth, held me close to my mother's breast, fed me, and
> kept me warm. They have protected me in times of danger and
> consoled me in times of grief. They have waved me good-bye
> and always welcomed me back. Those hands are God's hands.
> They are also the hands of my parents, teachers, friends, heal-
> ers, and all those whom God has given me to remind me how
> safely I am held.[6]

All of us are like that son, needing more desperately than anything else the strong and gentle embrace of the hands of God. We must be those hands for each other—not someday, but today. Rembrandt painted the father's hands shortly before his death. Nouwen himself was en route to The Hermitage at St. Petersburg in 1996 to make a film about the Rembrandt painting when a heart attack robbed him, far too young, of life. Life is tenuous and fragile.

George Eliot was right: "When death, the great Reconciler, has come, it is never our tenderness that we repent of, but our severity." Let us be gentle with each other. Let us touch each other. Let us touch even those who seem in some superficial way to be different. For we are all of us sons and daughters of God.

TOUCHING HANDS

I once heard Peter Storey, preaching in Johannesburg during the reign of apartheid, suggest that we should be prepared when we sing that old child's hymn: "Into my heart, into my heart, come into my heart, Lord Jesus." Storey imagined that Jesus' reply would be, "Okay, here I come, but I'm bringing all these other people with me."

God has fashioned a delightful tapestry of diverse people on this planet. It is only when we recognize our spiritual kinship that we can celebrate and honor that glorious array of humanity. In heaven there will be no sections, no divisions, no sides, no class, just people, with Jesus. Maybe we should start getting used to how things eventually are going to be.

Whom can you touch today? Yours are hands with which Christ is to touch now.

HEALING HANDS

Then some people came,
bringing to him a paralyzed man,
carried by four of them. (Mark 2:3)

In the earliest days of Christianity, even the greatest skeptics acknowledged that Jesus was a healer. In his journeys around the Galilean hillsides, he touched people and they were somehow healed of various maladies, such as blindness, leprosy, lameness, and others that we might diagnose as mental illness (viewed in the ancient world as demon possession). A single Gerasene man was afflicted by a legion of demons, and Jesus sent them into a herd of swine (Mark 5:1-20). He touched the daughter of Jairus (Mark 5:41); he applied saliva, and in another case, spittle and mud, to blind men's eyes (Mark 8:23, John 9:6). With his fingers he restored a deaf man's hearing (Mark 7:33); by his touch he restored the severed ear of the high priest's slave (Luke 22:51).

PRAYERS FOR HEALING

Somewhat surprisingly, in our era of medical sophistication, with our intricate knowledge of the body and our ability to combat disease with medication and surgery, we still have people called "faith healers," who feel they are continuing the work of healing begun by Jesus. While some such healers have been exposed as charlatans, there is widespread belief that, at least on a few occasions, prayer and the laying on of healing hands can effect miraculous cures. Pilgrims flock to shrines such as Lourdes, and countless Christians in hopeful humility raise their plaintive voices in a mighty chorus of prayers for the sick each day.

We spoke in chapter 2 about the sad but inevitable truth that many prayers simply are not "answered," that all the sick are not healed, that praying for healing can be an exercise in frustration. And yet these prayers are never entirely futile. Madeleine L'Engle tells of the long weekend she and her husband spent waiting for a biopsy result. She kept praying, "Please, dear God, don't let it be cancer." Someone suggested that her prayer was invalid: it already either was or wasn't malignant. But she wrote in her journal, "I can't live with that. I think we *can* pray. I think the heart overrides the intellect and insists on praying." She added, "If we don't pray according to the needs of the heart, we repress our deepest longings. . . . And so I pray as my heart needs to pray." Later, after cancer was confirmed and pronounced terminal, she wondered if her prayers had been wasted.

> Prayer is love, and love is never wasted. . . . Surely the prayers have sustained me, are sustaining me. Perhaps there will be unexpected answers to these prayers, answers I may not even be aware of for years. But they are not wasted. They are not lost. I do not know where they have gone, but I believe that God holds them, hand outstretched to receive them like precious pearls.[1]

Why not pray intently for healing? God wants us to pour out our hearts, to speak honestly, courageously, expressing our deepest desires and dreams. If we love someone, we can do no less. We gather up our relationship of love and offer it up into the hands of God. With undying hope we earnestly plead for a happy outcome. And when there is no happy outcome, we bow our heads in humility and join the ranks of those who know what Mark Helprin meant when he said this about God: "Being very clever, He has beaten life into a great question that breaks the living and is answered only in death."[2] We may even storm heaven with our questions and protests. And, at the end of the day we have surely deepened our fellowship, with God and with each other.

When followers of Christ join hands there is already a healing. For many, the most unspeakable aspect of suffering is feeling cut off from others. If we are to be the hands of Christ, perhaps our first challenge and privilege is not to perform dazzling cures through the laying on of hands, but to accomplish something more basic and ultimately of greater healing power: just to hold hands, lift up, hug—to create community.

THE HOME CHURCH

Consider the story in Mark 2:1-12, when four men hauled their paralytic friend onto a roof to be lowered to Jesus. The house belonged to Simon Peter's mother-in-law. Archaeologists have dug up a neighborhood of connecting homes from the time of Jesus in Capernaum. One particular house was like any other in most ways: stone walls, pottery and fish hooks lying around on the floor. But just a couple of decades after the death of Jesus, somebody put half a dozen layers of plaster on the stones. As time passed, religious graffiti were scrawled on the walls:

the names Jesus and Peter, and phrases like *Kyrie Eleison* ("Lord, have mercy") and Amen. This house may well have been the actual house where Jesus stayed and healed. Surely someone would have remembered the right house, and Christians would have set it aside for worship. In the fourth and fifth centuries, using this same house as its foundation, an octagonal church was constructed.

The image is riveting: a church built on the foundation of a home. Church ought to be like a home, in the best sense of the word: a place of comfort, a zone of acceptance, an atmosphere of unconditional love, a center of belonging. Robert Frost wrote that

Home is the place where, when you have to go there,
They have to take you in.[3]

We all feel in our hearts some nagging homesickness, a longing for home, a yearning finally answered only by God, but for now hinted at most profoundly in the life of God's people.

We need to encourage each other. Nobody gets too much encouragement. The power of a positive word, a loving embrace, a thoughtful note—these are all well within our grasp and abilities. Four people, with no miraculous powers of their own, brought that paralytic to Jesus.

Of course, the healing we are called to dispense may be physical— especially in our milieu. If we give more than a glance at the face of poverty, the potential for healing is unlimited. And it's achievable, through support of nutritional programs, more equal delivery of health care, the digging of proper wells, readier access to physicians and medicines, education, and the provision of hands-on assistance for persons in dire straits. Jesus healed with his hands. We are called to heal diseases, to be Jesus' hands.

A SILENT SIGN OF GOD'S PRESENCE

Whatever healing we offer, as Christ's followers we must be busy healing the most common and curable disease we all face: loneliness. After his wife's death from cancer, C. S. Lewis wrote poignant words about his anguish:

> No one ever told me that grief felt so like fear. I am not afraid, but the sensation is like being afraid. The same fluttering in the stomach, the same restlessness, the yawning. I keep on swallowing.
>
> At other times it feels like being mildly drunk, or concussed. There is a sort of invisible blanket between the world and me. I find it hard to take in what anyone says. Or perhaps, hard to want to take it in. It is so uninteresting.[4]

His next remark points the way for our ministry of healing: "Yet I want the others to be about me. I dread the moments when the house is empty. If only they would talk to one another and not to me."[5]

We have this terrible craving to do something, to fix things, to speak some magically effective words that will produce a smile and make everything okay. And yet, in times of real suffering, this is impossible. All we really can do is show up. And be there. The worst suffering is isolation, feeling cut off. We would love to raise Lazarus from the dead, as Jesus did. But we can do what Jesus did first. He showed up in

Bethany. He listened to the grief of his friends Mary and Martha. And he wept (John 11:35).

More recently, Cardinal Joseph Bernardin, just weeks before his death, wrote about his ministry to cancer sufferers. He suggests in *The Gift of Peace* that there is "a decisive difference between our pain as disciples and the pain experienced by those who are *not* the Lord's disciples." The difference is that "disciples suffer *in communion with the Lord*." Christ suffers with all who suffer, and this fact puts all suffering in a new light. In the meantime, all we can do, and strangely enough it is precisely what is needed, is to be present to those who hurt, to pray with them, to "become, in effect, a silent sign of God's presence and love."

GOD USES BROKEN THINGS

We are able to share the pain of others because, in the light of God's mercy, we know our own brokenness. Rainer Maria Rilke wrote a striking letter to a young poet friend in which he urged, "Do not believe that he who seeks to comfort you lives untroubled. . . . His life has much difficulty and sadness. . . . Were it otherwise he would never have been able to find those words."[6] We are all broken, wounded. And it is in precisely those places where we have been hurt that we can discover our giftedness. It is out of our pain that we can become healers. Our brokenness shows us that the cracks in our selves can become like windows, to let light in, and to let light out.

What is crucial is that we love—and that we love as God loves, indiscriminately, not based on our judgments of worthiness or even predictions of success. Mother Teresa was once asked about her sisters' involvement in caring for AIDS sufferers. She responded, "If there is a need God will guide you, as He guided us to serve those with AIDS. We don't judge these people, we don't ask what happened to them and how they got sick, we just see the need and care for them."[7]

In the end, healing as Jesus healed doesn't just help the person who is beleaguered. Healing affects relationships, overcoming alienation. Little wonder that Jesus was quick to talk about forgiveness in the same breath that he spoke of healing. We need to learn the healing power of forgiveness, to get beyond blaming. In a great scene in John Irving's *The World According to Garp,* Helen and Garp are terribly, painfully estranged, she having hurt him severely, both emotionally and physically. Unable to speak, Garp scribbles a note and hands it to her: "I don't blame you." After a few moments, he writes another note: "I don't blame me, either." Then he wisely adds, "Only in this way can we be whole again." We need this healing forgiveness, to forgive and to be forgiven.

HEALING HANDS

A few years ago, a friend of mine spent a week at Lourdes, the shrine in France where the Virgin Mary appeared to fourteen-year-old Bernadette Soubirous in 1858. Thousands of gallons of water flow from a spring there each day, and thousands claim to have been cured in its streams. When my friend returned, I asked her, "Did you see any miracles?"

She said, "Oh yes, every day."

"Every day? Tell me!"

She explained: "Every day at Lourdes, no matter who you are, or where you are from, or what's wrong with you, you are welcomed and loved."

A miracle. We have healing power in our hands. Can you see it?

What is in your hands that enables you to welcome, to repair, to encourage, to forgive, to love?

Yours are the hands with which Christ is to heal now.

FEEDING HANDS

Then Jesus took the loaves,
and when he had given thanks,
he distributed them to those who were seated; so also the fish,
as much as they wanted. (John 6:11)

J esus ventures to the east side of the sea of Galilee. A huge crowd, having gotten wind of titillating rumors of his mind-boggling powers, follows. The people wind up stranded, far into the day and country, without having packed anything to eat. A little boy is willing to part with his five barley loaves and two fish. Piece after piece is broken off until all five thousand are fed, and with more than just a morsel. A dozen basketsful are left over. Jesus fed the hungry.

GIVE THEM SOMETHING TO EAT

In Mark's Gospel, however, when the disciples state the obvious—that the crowd is hungry, that there is no food—Jesus pointedly deflects the request back at the disciples: "You give them something to eat" (Mark 6:37). The omnipresence of hungry people in our world is no secret; we can become almost bored with yet one more report of hunger in some seemingly faraway place, be it Somalia, Pakistan, the inner city. Yet the response of Jesus is the same: "You give them something to eat."

Being a Christian necessarily involves you and me in feeding the hungry. It is not heroic, but simply routine, normal, to bring canned goods for a local pantry, to deliver meals to the elderly, to dish out soup at a kitchen, to purchase livestock for another country. Since we are all kin in God's eyes, and since there is plenty of food on this good earth, we have an obligation to feed the hungry. It is intolerable for any person in the human family to languish without bread, to suffer malnutrition.

Even the smallest gifts make a difference. The little boy in the Gospels brings barley loaves. Barley was the staple diet of the poorest in the land. Persons of means had access to wheat loaves. So the boy not only gives, but he gives out of scarcity, not abundance. Mother Teresa tells of a beggar who said, "Mother Teresa, everybody's giving to you, I also want to give to you. Today, for the whole day, I got twenty-nine paise and I want to give it to you." She thought, "If I take it he will have nothing to eat tonight, and if I don't take it I will hurt him." She held out her hands and took the gift. "I have never seen such joy on any-body's face as I saw on his." The amount was so small Mother Teresa could buy nothing with it, but "it became like thousands because it was given with so much love." Those of us affluent enough to buy and read books need to hear Mother Teresa's challenge:

> You must give what will cost you something. This, then, is giving not just what you can live without but what you can't live without or don't want to live without, something you really like. Then your gift becomes a sacrifice, which will have value before God. . . . This giving until it hurts—this sacrifice—is . . . what I call love in action.[1]

THE BREAD OF LIFE

Jesus had an occasionally unwelcome habit of attaching a sermon to his miracles—almost as if he performed his wonder-working not so people would be impressed and receive stupendous benefits from his display of power, but so he could get their attention for what he really wanted to tell them. In John 6, Jesus feeds them, but moves on to talk about another kind of bread, his words, the bread of life (v. 35). "You cannot live by bread alone," he tells them—a frequent message on Jesus' lips. The people begin to exit, but he presses forward and begins to talk about death (v. 51), his death, their death, God's embrace of suffering. He shares the gospel.

Until Jesus fed the people, they could not hear his words. Missionaries have come to the same conclusion after decades of sending only preachers. Now we send doctors, agricultural experts, teachers, builders, and nurses. We begin by meeting glaring, present needs—and not just as a sneaky way to get a foot in the door! As I suggested in chapter 1, our first, primary, and perhaps final task is to care for God's world, and for the people in God's world.

Inevitably, a sermon, some word, is attached to each act of charity. If your church sends a team to serve a meal at the homeless shelter, you need not deliver a sermon or hand out tracts or Bibles. The very act of showing up and giving food is the most eloquent witness of which we are capable.

THE *FAUX PAS* AT TABLE

Mealtime for Jesus presented the most delicious opportunities to challenge people to rethink their priorities and behavior. He had a knack for committing a major *faux pas* at the table. Clearly, this Nazarene was untutored in gentility and the social graces. Invited to a sumptuous feast, Jesus turned on his generous host and quizzed him about why he had failed to include the poor, crippled, and blind (Luke 14:13). At another dinner he praised a loose woman who slipped in and poured exotic oil on his feet (Luke 7:44). Zaccheus, after Jesus invited himself to dinner, found himself repaying all those he had swindled—fourfold (Luke 19:8). "Miss Manners" would not have made much of an impression on Jesus.

The apostle Paul understood the peculiar meanings of meals and food. He sent the believers in Corinth, never a boring group, a stinging letter upbraiding them for their manner of sharing in the Lord's Supper (1 Cor. 11:20-22). When we think about Holy Communion in the early church, we have to remember that first, it was held in a home, probably one of the largest homes at the congregation's disposal; second, it was part of a larger meal; and third, it was leisurely, taking the better part of an evening. In even the finest Corinthian home, no more than twenty could be accommodated in the dining room. Since the church numbered perhaps sixty or more, the rest had to stay just outside in the atrium. What gets Paul bent out of shape is the social custom of the day: any respectable host seated the wealthy, persons of influence, inside. Furthermore, the wealthy always arrived first, with more leisure time, and consumed most—and certainly the best—of the food. The poor, working longer hours, could only arrive late and then be relegated to the atrium and the literal "leftovers."

For Paul this usual state of affairs was contrary to the nature of Christ and the church: all are welcome, all are treated equally. If anything, there is a preference for the poor, a kind of humility that offers the best seat and the finest portions to those who are usually denied or deprived.

The symbolism and power of the Eucharist change how we think about food, the breaking of bread, and who is welcome at the table. Once we have broken bread at the Lord's table, we cannot help but take bread out to those who have no bread at all. At the Lord's table, there is plenty of elbow room. We find ourselves sitting next to those who would normally be strangers. The hungry find themselves filled. The family of Christ shares fully in their father's board.

SAINT FRANCIS AT MONTE CASALE AND GUBBIO

Once three wicked thieves demanded food at the door of the friars' house in Monte Casale. Cognizant of their shady reputation, the guardian harshly sent them away. Soon Saint Francis arrived and heard of the encounter. He reproached the guardian for his behavior: "Sinners are brought back to God far better by kindness than by cruel reproofs." He compelled the guardian to find the robbers and carry several loaves of bread and a jug of wine to them, and to invite them to return as his guests. We are unsure who felt more awkward, the guardian or the thieves. Yet suspicion yielded to remorse and then reconciliation. Back at Monte Casale the thieves were received with joy and mercy—and after a few weeks all three became friars in the order of Saint Francis.

Another day, Francis journeyed to the village of Gubbio. When he arrived, the city gates were bolted shut, the citizens armed with knives and fierce looks. A wolf had been terrorizing the village. He had actually devoured several of the citizens of Gubbio! When a posse would venture up into the hills, the wolf would hide, or manage to eat one of his predators.

Francis said, "I must pay a visit to my brother the wolf." The citizens offered him weapons, but he climbed up in the hills unarmed, the citizens atop the city wall witnessing what they were sure would be the end of him. Sure enough, the wolf appeared, snarling, drooling, baring his fangs. Just as he approached Francis, the saint pulled out a cross from his pocket. The wolf sat down. Francis spoke: "Brother wolf, I hear that you have been a great sinner, that you have terrorized this village and have even eaten its inhabitants. This is a great sin against God! If you repent, you may be forgiven."

The wolf stared down toward the ground. Francis continued, "But I think I know why you've eaten the citizens of Gubbio. There is no food up in these hills. You are really just very hungry." The wolf looked up. Francis said, "I will make a deal with you. If you confess your sin, and promise not to terrorize these people any longer, I will get them to feed you every day." Francis reached down, and the wolf offered his paw in return.

At first the citizens of Gubbio were suspicious, on their guard. But after a time they began to trust the wolf. Brother wolf came in and out of their homes at his leisure. He was like a pet to them. Two years later, when he died, the citizens of Gubbio wept for days. And in 1873, workers repairing a stone floor uncovered a wolf's skull, elaborately buried beneath a chapel dedicated to Saint Francis.

In his book *I, Francis,* Carlo Carretto wisely concluded, "What is extraordinary in the incident of the wolf of Gubbio is not that the wolf grew tame, but that the people of Gubbio grew tame—and that they ran to meet the cold and hungry wolf not with pruning knives and hatchets but with bread and hot porridge."

Jesus fed with his hands, and now we are his hands, bringing food, hope, and peace.

FEEDING HANDS

One of the early followers of Saint Francis was Brother Juniper. So great was his love for the poor that when he saw someone with shabby clothing, he gave his cowl or habit to the person on the spot. Winding up clothes-less himself, he was commanded by his superior not to give his tunic or any part thereof to anyone. Later Juniper encountered a man who begged for alms. He replied, "My dear friend, I do not have anything to give you except this tunic and I cannot give it to you because of my vow of obedience. But if you take it from me, I will not stop you." Juniper was left standing naked. When he got home he told the other friars he had been robbed.[2]

Not only did Juniper give away his own clothes, but also the clothing, books, altar linens, and other items belonging to the other friars! When the poor came begging to Juniper, all the friars would jump up quickly and hide what they wanted to keep so that Juniper could not find them.

Hunger is everywhere. Hunger for food. Hunger for love. Hunger for belonging. Hunger for employment. Hunger for hope. Contemplate the creativity that Saint Francis brought to feeding people. Reflect upon the recklessness of Brother Juniper. What hunger can we satisfy? What is at hand to share? How can we feed the hungry of the world? Or in our community? Or even in our own home?

Yours are the hands with which Christ is to feed now.

SERVING HANDS

He poured water into a basin and
began to wash the disciples' feet. (John 13:5)

J esus said, "And whoever wishes to be first among you must be slave of all" (Mark 10:44). He also said, "As I have loved you, you also should love one another" (John 13:34). His best-remembered story was about a crime victim, left for dead, helped surprisingly by a detested Samaritan who embodied human compassion (Luke 10:29-37).

When it came to service, however, Jesus was never just talk. He was first and always a doer, someone who actually served. His entire life of service culminated in a shocking act: at supper, he poured water into a basin and washed the feet of his disciples. Jesus served real people. He served strangers, yes, and even those he knew best. One of Fyodor Dostoevsky's characters observed,

> The more I love mankind as a whole, the less I love individual people. . . . Whenever someone is too close to me, I feel my personal dignity and freedom are being infringed upon. . . . If I must love my fellow man, he had better hide himself, for no sooner do I see his face than there's an end to my love for him.[1]

Jesus saw faces, of real people, got close to them, and loved them.

THE DOCTRINE OF THE DEVIL

We live in a day when servanthood is curiously both in and out of style. Compassion, its twin, is generally out of fashion. But we do see fitful efforts at service. Businesses have suddenly discovered the value of service; companies who serve their customers well make plenty of money. This makes you wonder why you wind up waiting so long at the drive-through of a so-called "fast food" restaurant, or why a salesperson snaps at you. The truth is, people just don't naturally serve, even when it is in their own best interest.

On the other hand, lots of people see service as worthwhile, especially as something to include on their resumés. Individuals like to be able to claim their volunteer work. Corporations boast of hours and cash donated to community service. Again, though, the motivation is self-promotion, which isn't really service at all.

At its core, service is not something we do for ourselves. When it is self-motivated, it tends to be sporadic, performed only when convenient. This is what John Wesley called "the doctrine of the devil"—doing good when you feel like it. We have little bursts of good works at Thanksgiving or Christmas. But people are hungry in April, homeless in September, malnourished in July. Real service is regular, constant, normal.

Jesus served because he loved; he put others first. In Mother Teresa's biblical mindset, when we love others, we love Jesus:

> At the end of life we will not be judged by
> how many diplomas we have received

how much money we have made
how many great things we have done.

We will be judged by
"I was hungry and you gave me to eat
I was naked and you clothed me
I was homeless and you took me in."[2]

Service is not just something that happens in some far-off place. When Mother Teresa first came to New York, she told the crowd that you didn't have to go to Calcutta. Look around you, she urged, where you are, and find those who are hurting. And when you find them, love them. For in loving them, you love Jesus.

IDENTIFIED WITH HIS CREATURES

In these last two instances, Mother Teresa alludes to that speech Jesus made the last week of his earthly life. At the end of time, in the great judgment, the sheep will be separated from the goats. The lone criterion will be this: service. Did you feed the hungry? Give drink to the thirsty? Welcome the stranger? Clothe the naked? Visit those in prison? Those who did will share in eternal blessedness. Those who did not will be hurled into the abyss of eternal fire (Matt. 25:31-46).

Stern words. And frankly, this thinking seems to put Jesus squarely at odds with Saint Paul, who taught clearly that we are not saved by our good deeds, but solely by the grace and mercy of God. But Jesus adds to his story a double surprise. The first is that when we do these things for "the least"—for people who are down, hurting, disadvantaged—

then by the curious logic of the gospel we actually do them for Jesus. Jesus is in such solidarity with the poor, the downtrodden, the outcast, that he and they are really one.

The real test of our servanthood then is not just whether we care about poor folks down on their luck. The question becomes: Do you love Jesus? Since Jesus identifies totally with those who need compassion, to turn a deaf ear or to close your hand is in a profound sense a failure to love Jesus. In *New Seeds of Contemplation,* Thomas Merton put it like this:

> The more I become identified with God, the more will I be identified with all the others who are identified with Him. . . . The ultimate perfection of the contemplative life is not a heaven of separate individuals, each one viewing his own private intuition of God; it is a sea of Love which flows through the One Body of all the elect, all the angels and saints, and their contemplation would be incomplete if it were not shared.[3]

The second surprise is how the sheep respond to the news that they have been blessed with eternal glory: "Lord, when was it that we saw you hungry?" In the Sermon on the Mount, Jesus said, "When you give alms, do not let your left hand know what your right hand is doing" (Matt. 6:3). Genuine service has an absentmindedness, a spontaneity about it, a lack of self-consciousness or calculation. Through Jesus' teaching God has opened up for us an elusive but crucial paradox at the heart of our lives. The ultimate good in life is when we are liberated, let loose to become such lovers of God that we virtually surprise ourselves by loving those whom God loves, but freely, without expecting a payoff.

In 1847, just eight years before his premature death, Søren Kierkegaard wrote a beautiful meditation on compassion and service called *Works of Love*. He composed elegant harmonies and variations on those melodies of the Bible: that love is not just a feeling but a duty, that our love begins in God's love, that love can never be assumed but is always at risk. One of his most remarkable admonitions was this:

> Beware that it does not become more important for you that you are looked upon as loving them than that you love them; beware that your being loved does not become more important for you than that wherein you ought to love each other; beware that they do not trick you out of the highest because you cannot bear to be called selfish.[4]

We will falter. Our motives will never be wholly pure. But we serve, not so we can pat ourselves on the back for our nobility, but as a natural (even supernatural) reflex of the love of God living in us, working through us.

We may not succeed. But success is never the measure. We serve because that is just how it is with us and God.

THE SAVIOR LEAVES HIS IMPRINT

Service takes many mundane forms. In a culture that worships financial gain, money often lies at the heart of our service. At the same time, delivering human service to persons in dire straits is expensive. By some brilliant pairing on God's part, we need to give, which matches by no mere coincidence the skyrocketing expenses of helping people.

But money is not always the most important thing. A wealthy western woman visited Mother Teresa in Calcutta and offered to write a check to support the work of the Sisters of Charity. Mother declined: "I won't take your money." The woman insisted, reminding this human roadblock that she had great resources to donate. But Mother still said, "No money."

Exasperated, the woman stammered, "Well, what can I do?"

Mother said, "Come and see." She led the woman by the hand down into a dreadful barrio, found a desperately dirty, hungry child, and asked the woman to take care of him. Her pocketbook being of no avail, the woman took a cloth and water basin and bathed the child. Then she spooned cereal into the child's mouth. The woman reported later that her life was changed. She became part of something money could not buy, fix, or replace. Servanthood is human, personal, tangible. *Come and see.*

One of the relics housed in St. Peter's Basilica in Rome is the so-called "veil of Veronica." Who was Veronica, and what is this veil? In Luke 23:27 we find the moving detail that, while Jesus carried his cross toward Golgotha, many women followed and wept for him. The Catholic tradition has ritualized the movement toward crucifixion in the Stations of the Cross. The sixth station preserves a bit of ancient lore that one woman broke through the cordon and wiped Jesus' face with her veil. The name traditionally given her, Veronica, means "true image." A small gesture, this wiping of his face. But she did what she could. Karol Wojtyla, before his elevation as Pope John Paul II, wrote that "the Saviour leaves his imprint on every single act of charity, as on Veronica's handkerchief."[5]

SERVING HANDS

Even those outside the church comprehend the value of servanthood. Robert K. Greenleaf wrote a marvelous book, *Servant Leadership*, in 1977. He persuasively argued that all great leaders are servants first and always. People respond best and perhaps only to those who have proven themselves trustworthy as servants. Companies and institutions are foolish to fail to keep servanthood as the fulcrum of all they are about. If listening, empathy, and taking into account people's needs and limitations can be regarded as crucial in business, how much more should followers of Christ be noteworthy primarily for their humble, compassionate service of others?

I read that Mother Teresa once said that if at the end of the day you want to examine your conscience, just look at your hands. What have your hands done today? Whom have they served? Has the imprint of Christ's image been left on anything those hands have touched?

Yours are the hands with which Christ is to serve now.

HOLY HANDS

Jesus bent down and wrote
with his finger on the ground. (John 8:6)

Jesus' hands were holy hands. He was "tested as we are, yet without sin" (Heb. 4:15). But the religious people of Jesus' day certainly didn't think so. He stepped over too many of their time-honored boundaries demarcating what was holy and what was not.

This is what Jesus was up to: through his words and actions he was craftily redefining a new kind—a truer kind—of holiness. In Jesus' day, holiness was well defined and carefully prescribed. Rules meticulously delineated what was pure or impure, what was sacred or profane. Many Jews clung to their identity through these regulations of behavior, diet, and routine. Those who stepped outside the boundaries bore the stigma of "sinner," outcast.

Jesus, however, was not primarily a teacher of ethics; he did not systemize a new set of rules for a life pleasing to God. We might say his ministry did not encourage conformity—trying to adhere to a set of rules. Rather his ministry focused on transformation—embracing a vision that enabled people to enter into a new kind of life (Rom. 12:2).

THE CIRCLE OF HOLINESS

One Sabbath day, the disciples were hungry, and Jesus let them eat grain from a field. Questioned by the Pharisees, Jesus responded with what must have seemed a loose interpretation of the law: "The sabbath was made for humankind, and not humankind for the sabbath" (Mark 2:27). But it is not that Jesus was loose. If anything, he cut to the core of what a law was about, thereby radicalizing it. In the Sermon on the Mount, for example, Jesus excavated his audience's souls. To all who had never murdered, he reminded them that anger is a lethal killer (Matt. 5:22). To those who technically had never committed adultery, he excavated deep into their souls and uncovered lust as the heart of adultery (Matt. 5:28).

Boundaries were redrawn—and obliterated. Jesus was despised largely because he chose to sit down with persons outside the circle of holiness: a Samaritan woman, tax collectors, harlots. Jesus talked and behaved as he did in order to trip us up in our perpetual rush to judgment. If lust equals adultery, most of us cannot look down our moral noses at an adulterer. If Jesus sat with harlots, why are we so discriminating about the company we keep? Saint Augustine said knowingly that the sword of judgment, even as it is directed at some other person, first passes through your own heart.

Holiness is not the formation of an elite club of do-gooders. Jesus' kind of holiness was all about compassion, a new, inclusive fellowship. To use John Wesley's words, holiness is both internal, purity of heart within, and also external, the manifestation of that holiness in acts of love toward others in need.

A HARSH BONDAGE

Yet Jesus' compassion and fellowship were far from an endorsement of any and every lifestyle. There is something delicate about holding together the notion of compassion and unconditional acceptance of all people, with the seemingly incompatible notion of having standards and taking a firm stand on right and wrong. F. Scott Fitzgerald said the sign of real intelligence is being able to hold two contradictory opinions at once; Winston Churchill famously admitted that he believed being right was preferable to being consistent. Undying compassion and high standards: gritty intelligence, vision, and courage are required to hold them together.

Yet Jesus did—by bearing the world's sins and openly inviting all people into another kind of life. To the woman caught in adultery Jesus said, "Go your way, and from now on do not sin again" (John 8:11). This sounds a bit simplistic—as if people can just go out and suddenly be different, avoiding the habits of sin they have spent a lifetime cultivating! It was Augustine who recognized that "when lust is served, it becomes habit, and when habit is not resisted, it becomes necessity. By such links, joined one to another, as it were—for this reason I have called it a chain—a harsh bondage."[1] This is why those naïve "Just say no!" campaigns against sex and drugs are so ineffectual. The problem is precisely that you are utterly unable to grit your teeth, say no, and do good.

If we are to be holy, some other force must intervene. But how does God intervene to make us holy?

TURNING THE CENTRAL PART OF YOU

Holiness probably begins in recognizing that it is achieved, if at all, over time, through training, a long process of little decisions and adjustments of thought. C. S. Lewis was on the mark in *Mere Christianity:*

> People often think of Christian morality as a kind of bargain in which God says, "If you keep a lot of rules I'll reward you, and if you don't I'll do the other thing." I do not think that is the best way of looking at it. I would much rather say that every time you make a choice you are turning the central part of you, the part of you that chooses, into something a little different from what it was before. And taking your life as a whole, with all your innumerable choices, all your life long you are slowly turning this central thing either into a heavenly creature or into a hellish creature: either into a creature that is in harmony with God, and with other creatures, and with itself, or else into one that is in a state of war and hatred with God, and with its fellow-creatures, and with itself. To be the one kind of creature is heaven: that is, it is joy and peace and knowledge and power. To be the other means madness, horror, idiocy, rage, impotence, and eternal loneliness. Each of us at each moment is progressing to the one state or the other.[2]

To become a heavenly chooser, much must be learned—and practiced. Philosophers as far back as Socrates and Aristotle recognized that life is not about the satisfaction of desires. We do not emerge from the womb desiring the right things. Virtue must be learned. This is why we must be exceedingly vigilant about what we soak into our brains as we go through life. Watching television, or reading the tabloids, may poison our selves. Behaviors that once were unthinkable are now generally accepted in our culture simply because of constant exposure in the media. I'm not saying that we should be Pollyannas, eschewing anything that cannot pass some litmus test of niceness. But we do need to be careful about the shaping of who we are and how we react to what we see and hear.

The influence of others is essential. Who do we think is cool? Who are our exemplars? As a child, I spent hours on my backyard court mimicking the form and moves of Jerry West and Earl "the Pearl" Monroe; that's how you learned to play basketball. Whom are you imitating with your life—even if unwittingly? I know a saint in my community, and I am watching him, copying his little moves, his humility, his gentleness. We may even get so serious about holiness that we will enter into covenants with others to hold each other accountable—as did the early Methodists.

Holiness is more than just having the right position on big moral issues. Holiness is more mundane—how we deal with little situations, every day, not just when we stumble into some quandary. And the objective is eventually to learn to take pleasure in holiness. Aristotle taught that genuine pleasure is found only in the life of virtue. We miss the whole point when we live trying to balance pleasure over against virtue: "I'll deny myself some pleasure to be good." The pleasures of holiness, once grasped, are the deepest, most exhilarating, and most enduring.

TO BE NORMAL

To become holy is really a recovery of our truest, oldest self as intended by God. An interviewer once asked Mother Teresa, "Why are you so holy?" She responded: "You sound as if holiness were weird, or abnormal. To be holy is to be normal. To be anything else is to be abnormal."

We need more normalcy. To pursue that twin holiness John Wesley described, inner holiness (the purity of our own thoughts and habits) and outer holiness (exhibiting a life devoted to God through acts of charity), is not some quirky heroism. Inner and outer holiness is just normal.

And we will never be totally pure. The truer holiness taught by Jesus did not refrain from getting messy in the realities of the world. This genuine holiness could even be called reckless. Reinhold Niebuhr once said there can be a crucial difference between those who want to be pure, and those who want to be responsible. When we get involved, when our hearts are impassioned to be about spreading holiness in the real world, our hands and clothes will inevitably get messy. The quest for holiness is forever incomplete and can never be an excuse for irresponsibility regarding the realities of life in God's world.

THE RESISTANCE OF TIGHTLY CLENCHED FISTS

Holiness requires letting go, making some space. Maggie Ross suggests in her book, *The Fountain & the Furnace*, that we feel empty not because we are empty, but because we are full of the wrong stuff. This is why fasting and abstinence have been crucial in the history of Christian devotion. It is not that abusing yourself is somehow noble, or that the things of this world are evil. Rather we are constantly titillated with this and that, this pleasure, that taste, this image, that sound, and over time our sensitivity to the highest goods is dulled. We settle for less than God wants. Or else our lives are just too crammed full of stuff, and we need to make room.

Henri Nouwen wrote that "resistance to praying is like the resistance of tightly clenched fists," telling of an elderly woman brought to a psychiatric center. Swinging wildly at any- and everything, the woman so frightened the medical staff that her doctor ordered everything to be taken from her. But in her fist she tightly gripped one small coin. It took two people to pry open her hand. She clung to it, Nouwen wrote, "as though she would lose her very self along with the coin."[3]

In the life of prayer, "you discover you don't want to let go. You hold fast to what is familiar, even if you aren't proud of it. You find yourself saying, 'That's just how it is with me. I would like it to be different, but it can't be now.'"[4] When we talk this way we simply pass up the opportunity to live a truer, more holy life.

But the possibility is ours—or rather, it is God's. John Wesley taught that sanctification is a gift, something the Spirit of God does inside us. We prepare and hope for the gift by discipline, by avoiding what is unholy, by surrounding ourselves with holy images and conversations, by prayer, and even by fasting. We make the small decisions and adjustments Lewis described. But in the end, a new life, the true life we were made to live, is pure gift.

HOLY HANDS

But even a pure gift is easy to miss. In *The Power and the Glory,* Graham Greene tells of an old priest noted mostly for drinking whiskey and a string of failures. He finds himself in the last morning of his life: "What an impossible fellow I am, he thought, and how useless. I have done nothing for anybody. I might just as well have never lived." And then Greene offers this haunting verdict:

> He felt only an immense disappointment because he had to go to God empty-handed, with nothing done at all. It seemed to him, at that moment, that it would have been quite easy to have been a saint. It would only have needed a little self-restraint and a little courage. He felt like someone who has missed happiness by seconds at an appointed place. He knew now that at the end there was only one thing that counted— to be a saint.[5]

How empty-handed are you? Where is some self-restraint needed? What do you need to let go of to be holy? When does some courage need to be mustered? How can new habits be developed so that you might be more "normal"? Yours are the holy hands of Christ.

PIERCED HANDS

He was wounded for our transgressions. (Isaiah 53:5)

N ow that we have reflected on all the marvels Jesus did with his hands, we turn to the most vital thing we can say about the hands of Jesus. It is not anything his hands did, but rather what was done to them. In the spring of A.D. 30, just outside a western corner of the wall around Jerusalem, Jesus' hands were pierced, nailed to a wooden crossbeam, in a gruesome, horrific, public execution.

WHY DID THEY KILL HIM?

The brutality of crucifixion has been underlined by the discovery of the remains of a young man who lived during Jesus' time. His skeleton lay in an affluent cemetery just outside Jerusalem at Givat ha-Mivtar. A seven-inch nail still protruded through his heel. This unknown man and Jesus both suffered crucifixion, a humiliation reserved for the despicable: slaves, mutinous soldiers, and outcasts.

Somehow, though, the tragic wounding of Jesus' hands was transformed into the ultimate manifestation of God's love for us, and of our hope in God. Of course, to be historically accurate, the nails were not driven through the hands, but into the wrists. Yet the legacy of Christian art and hymnody has focused on his hands. Whether in our minds we hold on to the traditional image of pierced hands, or to the no less poignant picture of a hand, writhing in pain, arched just above a pierced wrist, we are repelled by and yet strangely drawn to this man who willingly accepted this shameful sentence out of his commitment to God and to you and to me.

Why was it necessary for those hands to be pierced, for Jesus to suffer ignominy? The pat answer, "for our sins," is true, but troubling. Dorothy Sayers, the brilliant mystery writer, portrays the bad theology that can emerge from this kind of thinking:

> God wanted to damn everybody, but his vindictive sadism was sated by the crucifixion of his own Son, who was quite innocent, and, therefore, a particularly attractive victim. He now only damns people who don't follow Christ or who have never heard of Him.[1]

But the God of the Bible simply isn't a power-hungry autocrat whose game is power, guilt, and punishment, who values his honor above human life. If Jesus taught us anything, it is that God is humble, compassionate, not the tit-for-tat type at all.

So why did Jesus die on the cross? Let's alter the question: why did they kill him? They didn't kill him so their sins could be forgiven! Rather, they killed him for much of what he did: touching the wrong people, teaching subversive ideas, shaking up the status quo, threatening the powers that be. In short, his dogged commitment to his mission, a mission of love for all people, put him on a collision course with the authorities, and they got rid of him.

TWO GRACES

We need to ponder that commitment. In the final months of his life, Saint Francis of Assisi prayed these remarkable words:

> My Lord Jesus Christ, I pray you to grant me two graces before I die. The first is that during my life I may feel in my soul and in my body, as much as possible, that pain that you, dear Jesus, sustained in the hour of your most bitter Passion. The second is that I may feel in my heart, as much as possible, that great love with which you, O Son of God, were inflamed in willingly enduring such suffering for us sinners.[2]

Jesus knew sorrow and even death. Many Protestants prefer to think about the risen Christ, up and walking about, elevated to glory—because we don't like to think about our own mortality. As Woody Allen put it, "I would like to achieve immortality without dying." But all the great spiritual writers in history coax us mortals in the direction of the cross: Paul, Augustine, Gregory, Anselm, Eckhardt, Luther, Teresa of Avila, John of the Cross, and in our own century, Barth, Merton, Nouwen—the list goes on. God shows himself to us, but in no obvious way. God is hidden—there, to be sure, but hidden. And it is in precisely the moment that seems to contradict God's divinity that God is most divine, or most clearly known.

The cross proves to be a window flung open into the very heart of

God. God's heart reveals itself to be one of pure compassion, immense, immeasurable love, unstinting mercy. On the cross, Jesus took on his own heart all our sin, all our false starts, all the debris of our lives, all our hurts, those inexplicable tragedies, our rejection, our grief, all human hopelessness, every tear.

The cross itself, if it was constructed of olive wood, the most abundant wood near Jerusalem, must have been less artistically exquisite than the crosses we erect in our churches. Olive wood bends and twists, with knots and crooked joints. The cross of Christ may be imagined as a gnarled shaft of a tree, bent in our spiritual imagining in the shape of a question mark, God's question mark, looming over our existence, reminding us that things are not as they seem. Yet it also looms over all cynicism and despair, asking: What disaster is so great that God has not entered into it fully and known it entirely?

WHERE IS GOD NOW?

Elie Wiesel tells the story of that darkest of nights when the SS officers of Auschwitz took a young boy, somebody's son, tied a noose around his neck, and kicked out the chair beneath him. As Wiesel watched the boy strangling to death, he heard a voice behind him asking,

> "Where is God now?"
> And I heard a voice within me answer him:
> "Where is He? Here He is—He is hanging here on this gallows. . . ."[3]

Some have misunderstood Wiesel to be saying there is no God;

how could there be a God if such evil things are allowed to happen? But Wiesel was saying that God was there, that God took all that agony into his own heart, bearing his people's sorrow.

That's really what Christ did on the cross. He took upon his own heart all evil, all our suffering. God put his loving arms around our pain. God filed a painful protest against evil. And God announced in Jesus' flesh and blood that evil does not have the final say. God has the last word, and that last word is one of hope, one of redemption.

One with us in our pain, God is not aloof from our existence, is not divorced from what is ugly. We never really die alone! God is there in the midst of our suffering, surrounding our pain, ennobling our agony, sharing it all as his own.

For us, it is all joy and hope to rest in that mercy. Our souls perhaps could nowhere be better nourished than by the discipline of simply looking at a crucifix. Karl Barth hung a print of the Isenheim altarpiece above his desk. Frederick Buechner's *Faces of Jesus* contains some startling images of the crucifixion from various cultures. Many Protestants would object to this suggestion, saying, "We believe in the empty cross!" But in all four Gospels, the moment of revelation, the real breakthrough of God's love, comes at the point of Jesus' death. Even after the resurrection, Jesus still bears the scars from his brutal killing.

Jesus' pierced hands are extensions of the heart of God, a heart overflowing with compassion and love.

TO BEAR THE BEAMS OF LOVE

Think again of the gnarled cross as a question mark. Jesus in his suffering stands forever as God's challenge to us, questioning our values, our foolish quests, our lack of compassion, our self-centeredness. The cross is God's reminder that you don't resolve conflict by force but by love, that integrity is costly but is ultimately honored by God, that those with clout are more likely to be in the wrong than the weak are.

On Passover, traditionally at least half a million lambs were slaughtered in a veritable bloodbath. All this killing was no doubt something like a lesson in living. God wanted us not to be so materialistic, so God required that we voluntarily give up a lamb, or a ram, not just to be burned for our own good but given to the needy who had no lamb at all. And if you know it will cost you your best ram or a lamb or goat, you'll think twice before hurting your neighbor.

In Robert Bolt's play *A Man for All Seasons,* Thomas More, who literally lost his head for his zeal to uphold God's laws in the courts of Henry VIII, asked, "Dare we for shame enter the Kingdom with ease when Our Lord Himself entered with so much pain?" Dietrich Bonhoeffer titled his most famous book *The Cost of Discipleship.* We prefer a cheap faith, something just added on, very comfortable, like a pillow. But the cost!

Becoming a Christian does not mean getting rid of our problems; rather, we exchange one set of problems for a new set, problems that are more challenging, yet more meaningful. Only one thing is more costly than discipleship—and that is non-discipleship!

The pierced hands of Jesus invite us to comprehend more deeply the sufferings of others. From his hands we understand suffering, and we see our oneness with all who suffer. Through his hands we are moved to share and even bear the pain of others. William Blake wrote, "And we are put on earth a little space, / That we may learn to bear the beams of love."[4]

PIERCED HANDS

The pierced hands of Jesus are the ultimate embodiment of God's love, the summons to love God that cannot be ignored, and the persuasive invitation to love one another. Find a painting or carving or photograph of a crucifix—not an empty cross, but Jesus hanging on a cross—and let your mind feel as deeply as possible what it must have been like for Jesus in his crucifixion. Consider his sorrow, his loneliness, his pain. Contemplate the depth of his love.

Remember that he endured all of this for you. And for those you love. And for those around whom you feel awkward. Those you dislike. Even those you do not know. Count the cost—to him, and to yourself, if you dare to follow. Learn to bear the beams of love.

The pierced hands of Christ.

SENDING HANDS

Jesus said to him,
"Feed my sheep." (John 21:17)

The Good News of the first Easter was that the grave could not contain Jesus. He was raised from the dead and appeared to his disciples. During those ethereal fifty days, Jesus' hands were active, noticed, touched. Thomas acquired his notorious nickname, "doubting," for his incredulity when the other disciples claimed to have seen the risen Savior. Jesus had mercy on doubters like Thomas. He gently held out his hands, still bearing the scars of his crucifixion, for Thomas to feel and believe (John 20:27).

On the road to Emmaus, Jesus caught up to a pair of distraught disciples, broke bread with them, and opened the scriptures to them (Luke 24:13-27). After a long night of fishing on the sea, the disciples caught a glimpse of him on the shore, cooking breakfast for them. After the meal, Jesus had a poignant conversation with Peter, the climax of which was Jesus' charging Peter with the task of tending and feeding Jesus' sheep (John 21:1-19). And before departing this earth, he no doubt raised those hands in one last gesture of blessing, sending his followers out into the world to make more disciples (Matt. 28:16-20).

A Cloud of Witnesses

Because of all that Jesus was and said and did, we cannot go about our business as usual. We are *called*. Jesus called fishermen by the edge of the Sea of Galilee (Mark 1:17). We may contemplate his hand beckoning with a gesture, inviting yet decisive, portrayed marvelously by Caravaggio in *The Calling of St. Matthew*. Jesus called many followers and sent them out to extend his work, to be his hands and feet (Matthew 10).

Today we often think of clergy as being "called." But God calls every person, not just ministers. Caravaggio recruited whomever he could, just out in the streets; the men he brought into his studio found themselves as disciples in his painting! Every person is called by God.

And God calls us not just to general niceness. No, God has something specific to which I am called, to which you are called. God wants me here, and not there. God wants you to do this, and not that. We are called to do something major with our lives (such as deciding whether to be a teacher or a custodian). We are called to do something seemingly smaller within today's schedule (such as reading to your daughter or dropping by a nursing home).

To comprehend the strange yet inestimable value of a *calling*, let's look back through history, listening to that great cloud of witnesses who have gone before us.

Late in the summer of 386, Augustine was struggling with conflicting thoughts in the garden of Alypius in Milan. He heard a voice, "Take up and read." He opened the Bible, took it as God's word calling to him, and became one of the great leaders in the history of the church.

In the village of Assisi, Francis was being groomed to follow in his father's footsteps as a wealthy cloth merchant. But after serving as a knight in the war with Perugia, languishing in jail for a time, and experiencing a series of dreams, prayers, and coincidences, Francis found himself praying at the crumbling, impoverished Church of San Damiano in the year 1206. Kneeling before the crucifix inside, Francis heard Jesus speak to him: "Francis, go and repair my house, which, as you see, is falling into ruin." His mission was not just to mend the broken masonry of San Damiano, but to repair the entire church and society of western Europe. God's call to this layperson revolutionized a whole culture!

In July 1505, an aspiring twenty-two-year-old attorney was struck to the ground by lightning. He burst out, "Help me, St. Anne, I will become a monk!" Martin Luther was jolted onto a path that led him to study and teach Bible and theology, to nail ninety-five theses on the Wittenburg door on All Hallows' Eve in 1517, to refuse to knuckle under at the Diet of Worms to the forces of the empire in April 1521, when he uttered his famous words, "Here I stand!"

On December 1, 1955, a seamstress boarded a bus in Montgomery, Alabama, and refused the demand of the driver, J. P. Blake, to yield her seat to white riders. Rosa Parks was called by God that day to stand up for her faith by saying, "Here I sit."

In 1977, Oscar Romero was chosen as the "safe" candidate for archbishop in El Salvador. But he refused to tolerate the repression and violence of the government, targeted so mercilessly against the poor. Authorities had him assassinated in 1980 while he was celebrating Mass.

John Wesley was a devout son of an Anglican priest, determined yet frustrated in his passion to be holy. In May 1738, already awed by the calm faith of Moravians and other Christians he had been watching, he stumbled into a meeting on Aldersgate Street and found his "heart strangely warmed" by the assurance that God's grace was genuine and very personal. His real calling, though, came when God nudged him out into the streets to proclaim the gospel to day laborers who would never set foot in any formal church building.

Dietrich Bonhoeffer had gotten out of Germany, seemingly in the nick of time. He could have continued making the rounds as a popular speaker in England and America, but he thought God wanted him back in Germany. He returned and was imprisoned and then executed in 1945 at Flossenbürg for his involvement in the attempt to overthrow Hitler.

On a train to Darjeeling in 1946, a young woman of no great distinction prayed and heard God telling her to reach out to the poorest of the poor. Mother Teresa and her Sisters of Charity have enveloped our globe with love.

My grandfather was a rural mail carrier. He sensed that this was what God placed him on earth to do, and he worked at it as if on a mission from God. He dispensed kindness with the mail, delivered medicine and groceries along with postal packages, and stopped to pray with persons along the way. He could have landed a better job elsewhere, but he had a keen sense of his crucial place in the functioning of the small town of Oakboro, North Carolina.

CALLING, NOT CAREER

These legendary stories seem strange today. We know little about the pursuit of a "calling"; our culture focuses instead on the pursuit of a "career." In a career the goal is more money, a higher rung on the ladder, a bigger office, and more plaudits.

But a calling is very different. Calling implies a function within the broader community, and in fact, a role in the betterment of the community. In the sentimental movie favorite, *It's a Wonderful Life,* the rich and corrupt Mr. Potter thinks he can buy off George Bailey with a fat salary, the nicest house in town, some new dresses for Mrs. Bailey, and the occasional business trip to New York. But George storms out of Potter's office back to his little building and loan, with little to show for his enormous efforts—except for a wonderful life and a different kind of Bedford Falls.

A calling has a moral purpose and is usually marked by sacrifice. Jesus warned Peter by the seashore: "Someone . . . will fasten a belt around you and take you where you do not wish to go" (John 21:18). Tradition has it that Peter was imprisoned and then crucified—upside down. From the very beginning, to embrace one's calling often meant the loss of something dear. Jesus did not come to the first fishermen and say, "Enjoy fishing; I'll see you soon." Rather he said, "Follow me," and they had to put down their nets to do so (Mark 1:18). The status quo, their very livelihood, had to be laid aside to pursue this highest calling.

Our whole culture cries out to you to abandon your calling and fall in line on the career track. Money talks all day long. People turn their heads just to glance at persons of position. "The good life" is defined as purchasing, possessing, enjoying. But God made each of us with a definite calling. In Susan Howatch's novel, *Absolute Truths,* Charles Ashworth wisely says, "It occurred to me . . . that hell was not, as Sartre had proclaimed, other people. Hell was being obliged to pretend to be someone quite other than one's true self." There is nothing more exhausting and hopeless than pretending. Only by listening for and doggedly pursuing our callings can we have any real energy and joy.

And yet there is nothing easy about doing so. You will have to lay aside more pleasurable tasks, easier diversions. Thomas Jefferson was an inveterate tinkerer, and loved nothing more than concocting some new gadget at his beloved Monticello. But he spent most of his life in Williamsburg, Philadelphia, France, and Washington. Why? "Nature intended me for the tranquil pursuits of science, by rendering them my supreme delight. But the enormities of the times in which I have lived have forced me to take a part in resisting them, and to commit myself on the boisterous ocean of political passions."[1]

To respond to your call, you need what Maggie Ross called "a willingness for whatever." This is not a divine boost along your pre-chosen path, but a total availability to God. This is our calling.

FEET OF INVINCIBILITY

If we look at the enormities of the times in which we live and take seriously the summons to be the hands of Christ, then we will find ourselves very busy, bumping up against the grain, with little triumphs and great frustration. Changing the world isn't something you can put on next week's to-do list. In *A Soldier of the Great War*, Mark Helprin tells of a wily World War I veteran who tries to share his wisdom with a young man who quickly grows weary as they walk along the road.

You may be tall, handsome, intelligent, graceful, and gifted;

but if you have feet of despair you might just as well be a dwarf who shines shoes on the Via del Corso. Feet of despair are too tender, and can't fight back. Under prolonged assault they come apart. They bleed to death. They become infected and swollen in half an hour. . . .

On the other hand, if I may, are the feet of invincibility. . . . Feet of invincibility are ugly, but they don't suffer, and they last forever—building defenses where they are attacked, turning color, reproportioning and repositioning themselves until they look like bulldogs.[2]

Clarence Jordan, a pioneer in race relations in the Deep South, had "feet of invincibility." Back in 1942, he read his Bible and thought he was supposed to put it into action. With a Ph.D. in New Testament Greek as well as a degree in agriculture, he developed Koinonia Farm, a pioneering cooperative venture where blacks and whites farmed, lived, and worshiped together—in Americus, Georgia! The price was constant harassment and sporadic violence. One night, the nearly ripened crops were burned to the ground. A reporter, who had actually participated in the KKK raid the night before, sought Jordan the next day for an interview. Mocking Jordan's education and apparent failure, he asked why he was out working that day.

Jordan looked up from his hoeing and responded, "We Christians aren't called to be successful. We're called to be faithful."

And we are called, like the community in rural Georgia, to be faithful together.

SENDING HANDS

Punctuating a little inlet by the Sea of Galilee, near the spot where Jesus commissioned Peter to feed his sheep, is an elegant statue. The firm but gentle hand of Jesus hovers over Peter, who lifts his hand in response. Imagine as best you are able the actual hands of Augustine, Francis, Luther, Parks, Romero, Wesley, Bonhoeffer, Jefferson, Jordan, my grandfather, and that someone in your life who embodies God's calling. These men and women sensed the power and the pain of the universe reaching out to them, and they went. What is your calling? What in particular are you being called to do?

Yours are the hands sent by Christ.

JOINING HANDS

A week later his disciples were again in the house. . . .
Although the doors were shut, Jesus came and stood among them.
(John 20:26)

Religious life in America today is a fiercely private affair. There is a secrecy, a dogged individualism about our faith, even among churchgoers. Increasing numbers of people feel they can be Christian without bothering with the church. We treat churchgoing like moviegoing. You check out times and locations, go, watch the show, come back if and when you feel like it, with no real expectation that you will develop any kind of relationship with your fellow moviegoers.

There are other kinds of Christians as well. Many go to church precisely to meet people, to make friends, even to extend business network tentacles. For many, the church is a nice place to do nice things with other nice people.

FUN AND JOKING

I talk with regular, involved churchgoers all the time who, when pressed just slightly, admit to being lonely. Anne Frank described her own experience in the introduction to her riveting diary:

No one will believe that a girl of thirteen feels herself quite alone in the world. . . . I have strings of boy friends, . . . I have relations, aunts and uncles, . . . a good home— no, I don't seem to lack anything. But it's the same with all my friends, just fun and joking, nothing more. . . . We don't seem to be able to get any closer, that is the root of the trouble.

We need more than fun and joking. We need real friends.

The genius of early Methodism was the small group. John and Charles Wesley saw the need for "societies," small bands or classes or cells of people, to meet for mutual encouragement and discipline. In 1743, John Wesley penned a description:

A society is no other than a company of men having the form and seeking the power of godliness, united in order to pray together, to receive the word of exhortation, and to watch over one another in love, that they may help each other to work out their salvation.[1]

Participation in such a group was no easy thing. When you arrived, after prayer and singing, you would be sternly questioned about your spiritual life. "What sins have you committed since our last meeting? What temptations have you encountered? Were you delivered? What have you thought or done or said that is sinful?"

For Wesley, one of the means of grace God has created for us is fellowship. Too often in church life, "fellowship" means lining up for a covered-dish dinner, eating too much, talking about the weather and sports, and generally having a lot of fun. But in the early Christian church, and in the Methodist societies, fellowship was much deeper, much harder, much more significant.

We are desperate for this fellowship. Our world is starved to see it modeled somewhere. We live among people who would agree with Jean Paul Sartre: "Hell is other people." We have forgotten how to get along. We are utterly unable to disagree with others. We get offended, we complain, we run and try to find little enclaves of agreement, people who are like us. But then we discover these people are different in some unforeseen way and we run from them, too.

FOR THE FRICTION

Scott Peck says we need other people "for the friction." Friction produces heat, heat we would prefer to avoid in our era of isolation. But friction also polishes, and we all have plenty of rough edges that need to be smoothed out, to get beneath the exterior to a shinier, beautiful self that can actually mirror the love of God in this world. Where else but in God's family could you wind up elbow to elbow with folks pretty different from yourself, and discover you not only must but do love them?

Jesus calls us into a new kind of family. In fact, throughout the Gospels, he displays a strange rudeness to his own family. Like any normal family, they grow concerned over the furor swirling around him. They worry he has gone out of his mind. So they come to Capernaum but cannot get into the house, such is the crowd. Word passes inside that the mother and siblings of Jesus have arrived. But far from having them ushered in for favored seating, Jesus dismisses their kinship and observes that "whoever does the will of God is my brother and sister and mother" (Mark 3:35).

For many of us these days "family" isn't a very friendly analogy. For all the talk about "family values" these days, we all know that the vast majority of families suffer from varieties of dysfunction. Leo Tolstoy's first sentence in *Anna Karenina* is on target: "Happy families are all alike; every unhappy family is unhappy in its own way." All too often, it is precisely the craziness of our family systems that compromises our ability to function as God's people.

ON FRIENDLY FIELDS

We need to redevelop our view of friendship and its purposes. In our culture, a friend is someone you enjoy doing things with, or perhaps someone with whom you share your troubles. But history bears witness to other kinds of friendship. In the 1930s, an impressive group of men began to meet in Oxford. C. S. Lewis, J. R. R. Tolkien, Charles Williams, Owen Barfield, and others, called themselves the "Inklings." They talked politics and religion, and read aloud what they were working on. Just imagine: a group of young men hearing Tolkien read the rough draft of *The Lord of the Rings* and Lewis trying out segments of *The Screwtape Letters!* The criterion for being in the Inklings was simply this: Do you care about truth? Members did not need to agree on the answers, but had to be passionate about the questions. Such a company of friends can be something like a school of virtue, in which we test our theories and practice doing good.

While superintendent at West Point, Douglas MacArthur composed these words which were carved on the stone entrance to the gymnasium:

Upon the fields of friendly strife

Are sown the seeds

That, upon other fields on other days

Will bear the fruits of victory.[2]

Within the body of Christ we need to be intentional about the seeds we sow, about how our behavior with friends should be preparing us for service out in the world. We need each other to draw us out of our self-centeredness. We need others to hold us accountable, to be like a mirror to help us see our lives and our doing of our faith more clearly. We need each other for mutual encouragement, to push further into serving the world than we might if left alone.

A LITTLE TENT

When God calls us to follow Christ, to be his brother, sister, mother, we discover a new way of relating, an alternate kind of family. Henri Nouwen suggested that many marriages "are like interlocking fingers":

> Two people cling to each other as two hands interlocked in fear. They connect because they cannot survive individually. But as they interlock they also realize that they cannot take away each other's loneliness. And it is then that friction arises and tension increases. Often a breakup is the final result.
>
> But God calls man and woman into a different relationship. It is a relationship that looks like two hands that fold in an act of prayer. The fingertips touch, but the hands can create

a space, like a little tent. Such a space is the space created by love, not fear. Marriage is creating a new, open space where God's love can be revealed to the "stranger": the child, the friend, the visitor.[3]

God calls us, invites us, yea, even pleads with us to be in community. We must create the kind of community that is fundamentally open, never a closed club of like-minded people who look alike. Partly, God's work is something you cannot accomplish alone. There's just too much to do. We have to learn again how to hold hands and work together, to be the body of Christ in this world. But we also have to realize that community *is* the work of Christ in this world. What God wants is for us to love, to share, deeply, and wisely. As we pursue this elusive goal, we will discover anew the presence of God in the real world in which we are immersed.

Frederick Buechner suggests:

Maybe the best thing that could happen to the church would be for some great tidal wave of history to wash all that away— the church buildings tumbling, the church money all lost, the church bulletins blowing through the air like dead leaves, the differences between preachers and congregations all lost too. Then all we would have left would be each other and Christ, which was all there was in the first place.[4]

A BURIAL SOCIETY

Scholars have studied how and why people got together in various voluntary groups in cities around the Mediterranean before the Christians arrived. A major function of such groups was to be a burial society. Persons made pacts with one another to pool funds to bury their dead.

Maybe the Christian revolution was not entirely different in purpose. For we are all mortal. We come together, not clinging out of fear, but holding each other up through even the darkest hours of suffering and death. Back in chapter 6 we saw the value C. S. Lewis placed on the presence of friends after the death of his wife, Joy. And Cardinal Bernardin spoke of the way we as a community function as a "silent sign of God's presence and love." The mystery of community is more than our trying to be Christ to one another; when two or three are gathered, Christ is there, among us, between us, around us.

And hope is there. Woody Allen once said, "I believe in eternal life. I'm just afraid nobody will tell me where it's being held." It's being held where and when mere mortals, entrusting their lives and futures into the hands of this Jesus who lived two millennia ago, join hands, reach out, serve, share, eager to be the body of Christ. Being the body is something I do, that you do. And yet it is a plural, collective concept. Being the body is something we do, that I cannot do by myself. We are the body of Christ.

JOINING HANDS

Though I have two left feet, I love music and the whole idea of dancing. I enjoy doing the Virginia Reel and those other utterly simple dances. If you can move, follow directions, and don't mind a few laughs, even the clumsiest dancer can participate. Any number of people can join in.

Being the body of Christ is like dancing the Virginia Reel. You certainly don't do it alone. You cannot do-si-do by yourself. You cannot swing your partner if you don't have one. The Christian life begins with the joining of hands, circling, moving together, urging that bystander into the joy of it all. And we may well imagine Christ standing and clapping in the midst of our circle, delighting in the dance.

The work of being the body of Christ is such that we cannot shoulder it alone. We need each other, our varied gifts, passions, and energies, working together, synchronized, encouraging each other. With whom are you called to be in fellowship? What will you do with the friction? How can we watch over one another in love? What will it look like when we help each other to work out our salvation? Yours together are the hands of Christ.

CONCLUSION

I therefore, the prisoner in the Lord, beg you to lead a life worthy of the calling. . . . There is one body. (Eph. 4:1, 4)

In 1956, decades before he was elected as Pope John Paul II, Karol Wojtyla wrote an eloquent poem about daily work that included these thought-provoking words:

Hands are the heart's landscape. They split sometimes
like ravines into which an undefined force rolls.
The very same hands which man only opens
when his palms have had their fill of toil.
Now he sees: because of him alone others can walk in peace.[1]

The landscape of Jesus' heart were his hands, split and full of toil. We have dared to take an imaginative look at what Jesus did with his hands and have seen in them an invitation to what we might do with our hands. For our hands are his. And our high privilege is to let them be used to reach up to him and out to others, so we and they may walk in peace.

WORK, WORTH, WORLD

Much has been left out of this little book. We could certainly go into more depth and develop a theology of work, as suggested in John Paul's poem. After all, Jesus was apprenticed to his father Joseph as a woodworker, and he knew more years in the humble routine of the carpenter's shop than in the ministry we see in the Gospels.

While we have touched on economic issues at every turn, we have not spoken directly of the ways our attention to earning and purchasing and consuming are so little consecrated to what Christ was about. Our grip on money and the stuff money can buy must be loosened significantly for us to be the hands of Christ. Jesus, who knew building, told that haunting story about the man who built bigger barns, only to die before moving in (Luke 12:13-21). Jesus himself, we may remember, was poor and owned nothing beyond the clothes ripped from his back outside that wall in Jerusalem. Jesus' hands were poor ones. How we think about broader economic issues, how we as a society tax and spend and prioritize, must matter to the God whose children are profoundly impacted by policy.

I have not mentioned ecology. Jesus could ask us to consider the lilies or the birds of the air in part because the skies over Galilee were clear. The past century's contribution to the atmosphere, earth, and oceans is an abomination. Each time a species is rendered extinct, a beautiful note in the great chorus of praise to God's glory, the created world, is silenced. We are charged with taking care of—not taking over—God's world, not using it on the whims of profit and pleasure.

Most glaringly I have said next to nothing about politics. When Jesus said, "Render unto Caesar the things that are Caesar's," he was not pleading for a disengagement from things political. Jesus, after all, was put to death because the authorities perceived, perhaps rightly, that he posed a profound threat to the power structures of the day. Admittedly, Christians throughout history have tended to be either embarrassingly apathetic about politics, or else embarrassingly engaged in politics, baptizing kings and wars and parties that are not of God.

But politics is about people, and we can hardly think about reaching out to the poor without contemplating and striving to influence forces in the political environment. And if we truly believe Christ is Lord of all, then we will inevitably find ourselves embroiled in political conflict. The cry to keep church and faith separate is often a mere subterfuge to keep things as they are. And it is the beneficiaries of the status quo who are loudest in support of keeping things as they are! During World War II, some Christians courageously stood up to Hitler. Martin Niemöller climbed into the pulpit and announced, "God is my Führer!"—and was thrown into a concentration camp. The Civil Rights movement was birthed when preachers in black churches saw clearly how the Bible itself screamed for changes in legislation and attitudes.

As we leap into the fray, we cannot foolishly seize upon one side or the other of the political debate as we know it. As Jim Wallis describes it, "We can find common ground only by moving to higher ground." As the body of Christ we must get involved in issues and policies that affect people. We may even be catalysts for a new kind of politics, focused on compassion and civility, a return to what previous generations knew as *citizenship:* people working together for the common good.

The truth is, no corner of life can be sheltered from the claims of Christ. All that we touch, all that bumps against us, all our stuff is to be gathered, offered up, and transformed into its place in the work of Christ.

IN CHRIST'S HANDS

We are to be the body of Christ. And yet, mercifully, perfection is not required. We know from the start that our embodiment of what Christ was about will be as flawed as our very own physical bodies, which are gangly, awkward, and always breaking down. Karl Rahner wrote truthfully that while the church has had its heroes, the church has never been all that heroic.

But we are Christ's body. We can be used in spite of ourselves. And it is perhaps when we fail most miserably that we make our most surprisingly eloquent witness to Christ. Of course we are not God. Otherwise there would be no need for God. And it is precisely our freedom not to have to be God, but to be ourselves, the people God made us to be, that liberates us to be, however awkwardly, and yet most definitely, the body of Christ.

Let us pray this prayer from that Anglican bishop from the turn of the seventeenth century, Lancelot Andrewes:

Lord Jesus, I give you my hands to do your work.
I give you my feet to go your way.
I give you my eyes to see as you do.
I give you my tongue to speak your words.
I give you my mind that you may think in me.
I give you my spirit that you may pray in me.

Above all,
I give you my heart that you may love in me,
your Father, and all humankind.
I give you my whole self that you may grow in me,
So that it is you, Lord Jesus,
Who live and work and pray in me.[2]

INTRODUCTION

1. Helen Keller, *The Story of My Life* (New York: Grosset & Dunlap, 1904), 23.

CHAPTER 1: LIVING HANDS

1. Henri J. M. Nouwen, *Here and Now* (New York: Crossroad, 1994), 18.
2. Douglas John Hall, *The Steward: A Biblical Symbol Come of Age* (Grand Rapids: Eerdmans, 1990).
3. William Wordsworth's poem "Michael" in *The Norton Anthology of Poetry* (New York: W. W. Norton, 1975), 593.

CHAPTER 2: PRAYING HANDS

1. Dietrich Bonhoeffer, *Letters and Papers from Prison,* ed. Eberhard Bethge (New York: Macmillan, 1971), 361.
2. Henri J. M. Nouwen, *The Genesee Diary* (Garden City, NY: Image, 1981), 139.
3. R. C. Byrd, "Positive Therapeutic Effects of Intercessory Prayer in a Coronary Care Unit Population," *Southern Medical Journal, Journal of the Southern Medical Association* 81 (1988): 826-829.
4. Robert McAfee Brown, *Liberation Theology* (Louisville: Westminster/John Knox, 1993), 88.

CHAPTER 3: UNFURLING HANDS

1. Jim Wallis, *The Soul of Politics* (New York: New Press, 1994), 21.
2. St. Athanasius, *On the Incarnation,* trans. and ed. by a Religious of C.S.M.V. (Crestwood, NY: St. Vladimir's, 1953), 96.
3. John Updike, *Rabbit Is Rich* (New York: Fawcett Crest, 1981), 226.
4. Allan Bloom, *The Closing of the American Mind* (New York: Simon & Schuster, 1987), 60.
5. *A Testament of Hope: The Essential Writings and Speeches of Martin Luther King, Jr.,* ed. James Melvin Washington (San Francisco: HarperSanFrancisco, 1986), 277.

CHAPTER 4: TEACHING HANDS

1. Alfred, Lord Tennyson, "The Charge of the Light Brigade," *Selected Poetry of*

Tennyson, ed. Douglas Bush (New York: The Modern Library, 1951), 254.

2. *The Collected Dialogues of Plato,* ed. Edith Hamilton and Huntington Cairns (New Jersey: Princeton University Press, 1961), 265.

3. Mark Helprin, *Winter's Tale* (New York: Pocket, 1983), 259.

4. Evelyn Underhill, *The Ways of the Spirit* (New York: Crossroad, 1996), 224.

5. Murray Bodo, *Clare: A Light in the Garden* (Cincinnati: St. Anthony Messenger Press, 1992), 85.

CHAPTER 5: TOUCHING HANDS

1. *A Testament of Hope,* 219.

2. Ibid., 220.

3. Ibid., 269.

4. Charles Dickens, *A Christmas Carol & Other Stories* (New York: Penguin, 1984), 35.

5. Elie Wiesel, *All Rivers Run to the Sea: Memoirs* (New York: Knopf, 1995), 354-355.

6. Henri J. M. Nouwen, *The Return of the Prodigal Son* (New York: Doubleday, 1992), 96.

CHAPTER 6: HEALING HANDS

1. Madeleine L'Engle, *Two-Part Invention* (New York: Harper & Row, 1988), 94, 186-187.

2. Mark Helprin, *A Soldier of the Great War* (New York: Avon Books, 1991), 662.

3. Excerpt from "Death of the Hired Man," from *The Poetry of Robert Frost,* ed. Edward Connery Lathem (New York: Henry Holt and Company, © 1958 by Robert Frost; © 1967 by Lesley Frost Ballantine; Copyright 1930, 1939, © 1969 by Henry Holt and Company), 38.

4. C. S. Lewis, *A Grief Observed* (New York: Bantam, 1976), 1.

5. Ibid.

6. Rainer Maria Rilke, *Letters to a Young Poet,* trans. M. D. Herter Norton (New York: W. W. Norton, 1954), 72.

7. Mother Teresa, *A Simple Path,* comp. Lucinda Vardey (New York: Ballantine Books, 1995), 87.

CHAPTER 7: FEEDING HANDS

1. Mother Teresa, *A Simple Path,* 99-100.

2. Murray Bodo, *Juniper: Friend of Francis, Fool of God* (Cincinnati: St. Anthony Messenger Press, 1983), 28.

CHAPTER 8: SERVING HANDS

1. Fyodor Dostoevsky, *The Brothers Karamazov,* trans. Andrew H. MacAndrew (New York: Bantam Books, 1970), 65-66, 284.

2. Mother Teresa, *Words to Love By* (Notre Dame, IN: Ave Maria Press, 1983), 80.

3. Thomas Merton, *New Seeds of Contemplation* (New York: New Directions, 1961), 65.

4. Søren Kierkegaard, *Works of Love,* trans. Howard and Edna Hong (New York: Harper & Row, 1962), 132.

5. Karol Wojtyla, *Sign of Contradiction* (New York: Seabury, 1979), 189.

CHAPTER 9: HOLY HANDS

1. *The Confessions of St. Augustine,* trans. John K. Ryan (Garden City, NY: Image Books, 1960), 188-189.

2. C. S. Lewis, *Mere Christianity* (New York: Macmillan, 1960), 86.

3. Henri J. M. Nouwen, *With Open Hands* (New York: Ballantine Books, 1972), 3.

4. Ibid., 4.

5. Graham Greene, *The Power and the Glory* (London: Penguin, 1977), 210.

CHAPTER 10: PIERCED HANDS

1. Dorothy Sayers, *Christian Letters to a Post-Christian World* (Grand Rapids: Wm. B. Eerdmans, 1969), 25.

2. Arnaldo Fortini, *Francis of Assisi,* trans. Helen Moak (New York: Crossroad, 1981), 557.

3. Elie Wiesel, *Night* (New York: Avon Books, 1960), 76.

4. From "The Little Black Boy," one of the "Songs of Innocence," *Selected Poetry and Prose of William Blake,* ed. Northrop Frye (New York: Modern Library, 1953), 25.

CHAPTER 11: SENDING HANDS

1. In Robert Dallek, *Hail to the Chief* (New York: Hyperion, 1996), 130.

2. Mark Helprin, *A Soldier of the Great War,* 18.

CHAPTER 12: JOINING HANDS

1. *John Wesley,* ed. Albert C. Outler (New York: Oxford University Press, 1964), 178.

2. William Manchester, *American Caesar* (New York: Dell Publishing, 1978), 135.

3. Henri J. M. Nouwen, *Here and Now,* 130.

4. Frederick Buechner, *The Clown in the Belfry* (San Francisco: Harper, 1992), 158.

CONCLUSION

1. Excerpt from *The Place Within: The Poetry of Pope John Paul II,* trans. Jerzy Peterkiewicz (New York: Random House, 1982), 64.

2. Lancelot Andrewes in Evelyn Underhill, *The Ways of the Spirit,* 101.